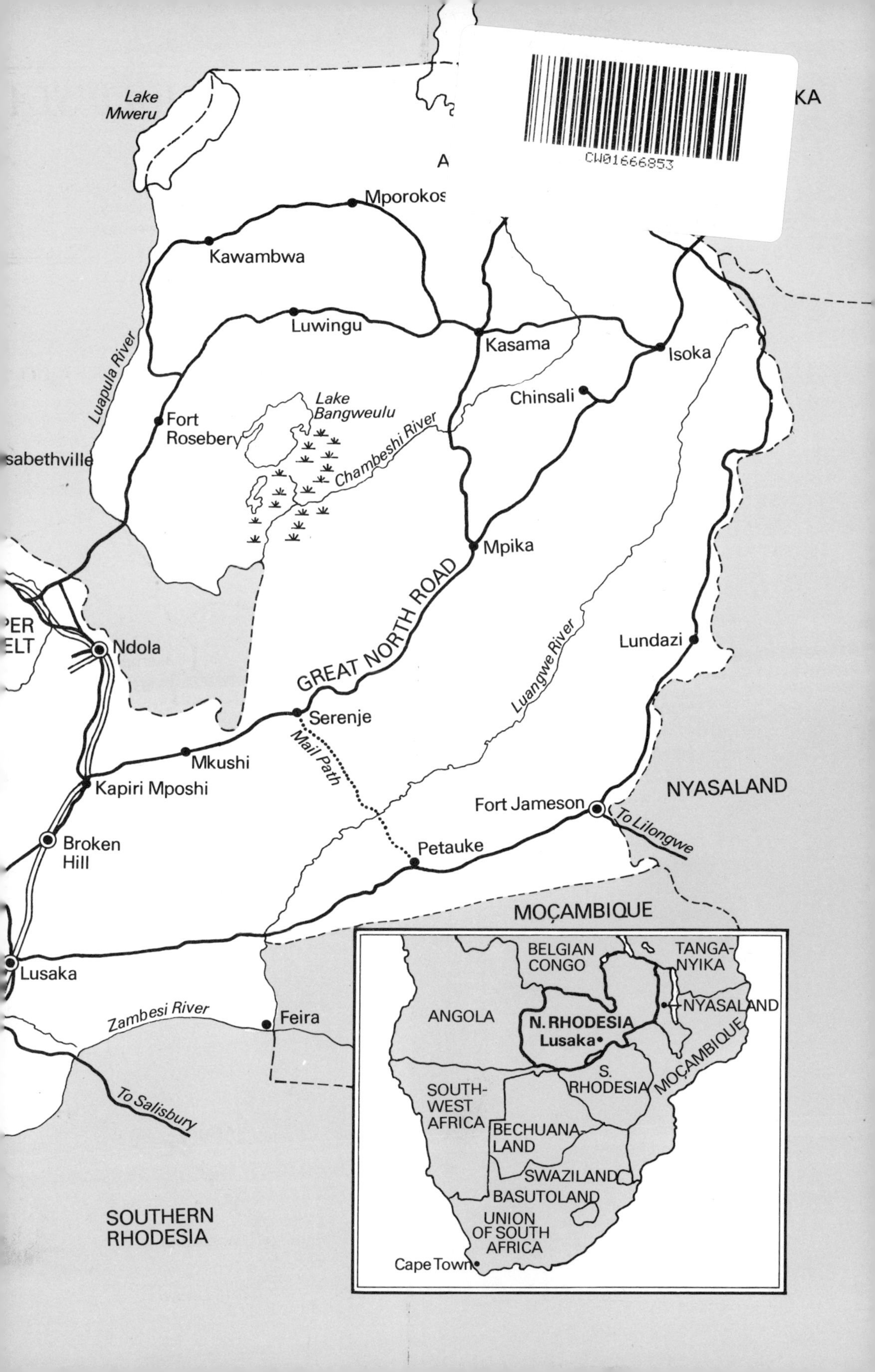

Lake Mweru
Mporokos
Kawambwa
Luwingu
Kasama
Isoka
Luapula River
Chinsali
Lake Bangweulu
Fort Rosebery
Chambeshi River
sabethville
Mpika
GREAT NORTH ROAD
Lundazi
Luangwe River
PER
ELT
Ndola
Serenje
Mail Path
Mkushi
Kapiri Mposhi
NYASALAND
Fort Jameson
To Lilongwe
Broken Hill
Petauke
MOÇAMBIQUE
Lusaka
Zambesi River
Feira
To Salisbury
SOUTHERN RHODESIA
BELGIAN CONGO
TANGA-NYIKA
NYASALAND
ANGOLA
N. RHODESIA
Lusaka
MOÇAMBIQUE
S. RHODESIA
SOUTH-WEST AFRICA
BECHUANA-LAND
SWAZILAND
BASUTOLAND
UNION OF SOUTH AFRICA
Cape Town
KA

THE FLAG-WAGGER

Other books by Harry Franklin:

Ignorance Is No Defence
Unholy Wedlock
Crash
Don't Go To Ceuta

THE FLAG-WAGGER

by
Harry Franklin

with an Introduction by
Elspeth Huxley

SHEPHEARD-WALWYN

First published 1974

ISBN 0 85683 006 2

Printed in Great Britain by
W & J Mackay Limited, Chatham

SHEPHEARD-WALWYN (PUBLISHERS) LTD.
56 Doughty Street, London WC1

Dedicated to all past members of the Colonial Service

CONTENTS

INTRODUCTION

THE WORDS 'colonial', 'imperial', 'empire', unless embedded in the names of chain stores or cinemas, are under a very black cloud. Even the least radical among the British shy away from them, and regard the former British effort to extend the *pax Britannica* over large parts of the earth's surface as at the best misguided, at the worst a heinous crime. The blush of shame has overcast the glow of pride. It follows that anyone who took an active part in the affair—spreading and maintaining British rule, standing to attention at sunrise and sunset when the Union Jack was raised or lowered, and believing that he had a mission to elevate the blacks—must be either a fool or a villain, probably both. Mr Franklin was one of this tribe. Those who read this account of how he carried out his duties in an African protectorate, then called Northern Rhodesia, from 1928 to 1951 will be able to judge for themselves whether this is an accurate way to describe him.

Truth is a chameleon, continually changing with its surroundings. In history there is not and cannot be objective truth. In this instance all one can say is that when Mr Franklin started his career the words 'colonial' and 'imperial' were not dirty words, the empire was a valid ideal and Mr Franklin and his colleagues, though they never actually wagged a flag, did regard it as a symbol of a good cause they were advancing to the best of their ability. The *pax Britannica* did not, for them, mean exploitation, ill-gotten dividends, oppression, and grinding the faces of the coloured poor; it meant helping peasants in the endless bush of Africa to become less poor, less downtrodden, less ignorant, less at the mercy of famine, superstition, tribal wars and oppression by dusky potentates. They doctored the sick, laid out the first primitive roads and bridges, tried and decided innumerable civil and criminal cases, conducted campaigns against such things as malaria and hookworm, and kept law and order so that others, such as missionaries and the specialist branches of the colonial government, could get on with the job of starting the first schools and dispensaries, inoculating cattle against diseases, introducing better methods of agriculture, combating epidemics and scourges like tsetse fly, and so on. All this they did on what it would be a gross overstatement to call a shoestring; Mr Franklin mentions that he was allowed £2 a month to pay the salary and expenses of a local treasury clerk.

He and his colleagues belonged to a *corps d'elite*. They were young men recruited in London, mainly from the public schools and older universities, and sent out to rule over vast areas of bush, forest, plain and desert, in the name of their Sovereign, as best they could. After a short apprenticeship as a cadet, they were sent as assistants to a District Commissioner who, perhaps himself not much above thirty, might have a region as large as half of England under his care. In Africa they went to a station known as the Boma, where there might also be a policeman, possibly a Public Works engineer or a Veterinary Officer if it was large enough, but very often just the D.C. They would spend, in those days, more than half their time on safari, camping by African villages and learning how the people lived and thought and acted, their languages, their needs. The villagers did not resent their presence in those bygone days. Quite the contrary. As a rule they accepted these white men cheerfully and without rancour as a kind of natural phenomenon from another world, and possessors of immensely potent forms of magic. Those peculiar strangers also collected taxes, which no one ever likes, gave judgements which the loser resented, and orders which might offend against deeply held customs and ways. So they were not uncritically accepted, but accepted they were, and respected and obeyed, especially if they had a sense of humour which bridged many cultural gaps. They were the chiefs, indeed superchiefs, and the peasants had not yet learnt to call themselves slaves. It was all very old-fashioned, Sanders-of-the-River-like, and today seems either incredible or absurd.

'Never', remarked the Spanish writer Santayana, 'had the world known such a just, sweet and boyish master' (or words to that effect). It was a remark which over-glamorized the colonial service, and the word 'boyish' strikes a chill to modern hearts. All the same he had a point which I think emerges from these pages. The colonial service was a corps of amateurs. They ran the world's largest empire on very little money, loving their work despite its drawbacks (these were many) and finding out how to do things as they went along. Mr Franklin, by no means a mechanically-minded man, invented a radio receiver which sold for £5, plus battery, because he found himself in charge of an excellent transmitter, but no one could afford the equipment to listen in.

Although his term of service in Northern Rhodesia spanned only thirty-three years, it ran from the halcyon days of 'yes, bwana' rule to the rise of the African National Congress, Sir Roy Welensky and the brink of the Federation of the two Rhodesias and Nyasaland, the disastrous consequences of which are with us to this day. He watched the hatching of African nationalism in the nest of the Second World War and its early growth, fed on the doubts and questions which arose in his own as well as in his colleagues' minds.

All this is clearly, tersely and above all humourously told. There is nothing in the least bit solemn about Mr Franklin's story. He is an individualist, often a rebel, sometimes a cynic, never a yes-man or respecter of persons. He can be very funny indeed. It is an honour, as well as a pleasure, to recommend his book. Readers will gain from it as clear and true a picture as they are ever likely to find of how once the all-but-forgotten colonial service ruled the defunct colonial empire, and of what sort of men they were. Above all, they will surely enjoy it. Whether or no Mr Franklin was once a flag-wagger, he is undoubtedly a wag.

October 1973 ELSPETH HUXLEY

CHAPTER ONE

The Flag-Wagger

AS A SMALL BOY I much enjoyed wagging my little Union Jack on Empire Day and joining in the song we sang at school for the occasion:

> 'What is the meaning of Empahyer Day
> Why do the cannons rawah?
> Why does the cry "God save the King"
> Echo from shawah to shawah . . . ?'

They were the only lines of the song I ever learned, so that the Poet Laureate's answers to these challenging questions were never known to me. But the tune was lusty, and the shrilling of several hundred voices lifted in excited pride and in the wondrous anticipation of hearing the Royal Artillery up the hill thunder a salute—the song was nicely timed to precede this—inspired me to da-de-da enthusiastically through the rest.

I knew the answers better than the Poet did anyway. I knew that we had put down slavery. I knew how Native potentates had implored and been granted Queen Victoria's protection; and how our brave missionaries, all over the Empire, were converting savage tribesmen to Christianity.

I dug a little deeper into history in the process of cramming for scholarships to carry me into a grammar school, and later to support me at the university. It was never my special subject, but I read enough of it to develop unworthy doubts in my mind as to the absolute perfection of the Empire. Some of the trade which had followed the flag, certain sources alleged, included commerce in cheap gin which had befuddled African chiefs and put them at a disadvantage in their negotiations with British Governments or chartered companies wishing to protect them. I also gained the impression that the war against the Boers was fought for gold and diamonds rather than for humanitarian reasons. But I consoled myself with the thought that one should expect some imperfections even in the conduct of the world's greatest nation. In any event, the era of conquest was long since ended, and that was comforting.

At Oxford I paid ten shillings to join the League of Nations, not of course as a Full Member. There was some kind of associate membership which attracted the more starry-eyed undergraduates of the time, the pacifists. We did not read much of the literature sent to us by the League—life was too full—but we felt that with the increasing support, both financial and moral, of the cream of Britain's young men the League would do a splendid job.

It was my father's teaching that had made me a pacifist ever since I was old enough to understand what he was talking about. The First World War had taken his favourite son. I was not, of course, a craven pacifist. I was prepared to fight anybody in the preservation of peace, which everybody agreed could be best ensured by a strong British Empire in firm alliance with America, which was more or less part of the Empire anyway.

It was clearly my duty to help to strengthen the Empire myself. I was well qualified to educate the turbulent savages somewhere: to turn them into splendid black Englishmen. That would make them very happy and ensure their loyalty to the Crown.

The task might be dangerous. The tribesmen might mistrust me at first. But with a revolver in one hand and a present of beads in the other, with kindness in my heart and a little band of faithful sepoys at my back, one carrying the Union Jack, I knew I would win them over.

I was led to this decision also by some other, less worthy, considerations. I found that I did not want to be, as I had originally intended, a mere schoolteacher. In my fourth year at Oxford I had taken a post-graduate Diploma in Education. My attempt to market it before I went down had been disappointing. The Leys School at Cambridge rejected me. The Oxford Appointments Board, flippantly known as the Disappointments Board, had insulted me with one proposal that I should apply to the Cunard Line for a job as a Purser's Clerk and another that I should take an American boy off his wealthy father's hands by tutoring him round Europe for an indefinite period.

Stung, perhaps, by my replies to these proposals, the Board then hopefully suggested that I might take a job abroad. Africa, they seemed to think, would not be too far away. They sent me a mass of printed information about the African colonies and a list of appointments vacant in the Colonial Service. I recognized the names of a few of the colonies and read up a little more about them in the Bodleian Library. Northern Rhodesia, I discovered, might become very rich in copper. It needed an Inspector of Native Education. I applied for the post and was accepted, subject to a satisfactory medical examination.

The elderly consultant physician to the Colonial Office who examined me beamed with delight when he observed, as I removed my trousers, that I did not wear sock suspenders. 'My boy,' he said, 'you will never get varicose veins.' The last hurdle was over. I thanked the old man and departed in a daze of wonder and delight. Here was I, young, pronounced to be in perfect health, free of varicose veins for life and with a marvellous job in His Majesty's Colonial Service. And a top job, right from the start. *The* Inspector of Native Education was the title of the appointment. There was only one. Me. Incredible. I forgave the Oxford Disappointments Board.

It was early Summer, 1928, and a beautiful day. I found myself wandering round St James's Park, my mind in Africa. I would have a uniform and a sword. The Colonial Office pamphlet said so. Only for ceremonial occasions, of course; not for inspecting schools. I tried to think of appropriate ceremonial educational occasions but none came to mind. I would be paid £400 per annum for the first two years, twice the pay of a schoolmaster. Then a rise every year. A bicycle allowance of a penny a mile. ('Curious, that,' I thought.) And there was an allowance of £30 for tropical kit before taking up appointment. I could probably save a bit on that. 'No, spend more' I thought. 'Buy the best.' The Colonial Service would be proud of me. So I bought the best tropical outfit and camp kit that Walters of Oxford could supply—on credit. It included a double-felted, sunproof-lined, four-gallon Texan hat with a brim that a Mexican would have envied. Nobody in Northern Rhodesia, I thought, would ever have seen such a fine hat before. Nobody had, as I later discovered.

The Colonial Office thought it wise that I should learn how to inspect Education before assuming responsibility for inspecting it in Northern Rhodesia and so they attached me for three weeks to a Board of Education Inspector visiting primary schools in London. He regarded my lack of understanding of the work, which was as total at the end of the three weeks as it was at the beginning, with fatherly indulgence. For a further three weeks I accompanied another Inspector on his tour of village schools in Essex. He expressed some surprise that I should be starting my working life with the rank of Inspector. Some years of teaching, he felt, would not have done me any harm . . . just as a grounding.

The only real knowledge I acquired during the three weeks in Essex was from a hotel waiter in Colchester. I wanted oysters and there were none. I protested that Colchester was the home of oysters. 'They all leave home and go up to London' he said.

Several months of inactivity followed. The Crown Agents sent me my pay, but it appeared that the Colonial Office had quite forgotten about me. I made the great mistake of writing to ask them when they would be sending me to Africa. They replied, asking me when I would like to go. 'As soon as possible' I told them. How young and foolish I was. I might have stayed in London for years, drawing my pay, while quietly pursuing some other profitable occupation.

The Colonial Office Educational Adviser had told me that I was urgently needed. I would be in on the ground floor of a tremendous expansion of education in the Protectorate. I found no evidence to justify either statement when I arrived in Northern Rhodesia, but I soon learned that theory in Whitehall and practice in Northern Rhodesia were as opposite poles, which yet attract each other and so maintain an invisible current which runs uselessly round and round for ever, unless directed to a practical task by interested electricians. We, of the Colonial Service, were the electricians.

CHAPTER TWO

Mostly at Sea

My enthusiasm for African adventure nearly sank in the Thames off Tilbury.

My mother had come to see me off. She was the most wonderful woman in the world. Naturally. She had been a village schoolteacher in the moors of Northumberland. If she taught the village children as she taught me, in such a way that you never knew you were being taught—you were just listening, wide eyed, to what she was saying—she must have done a marvellous job. She was tall and beautiful, patient and quietly, invariably, loving.

As the tender pulled away from the quayside and I waved my handkerchief, she was suddenly no longer tall. She had turned her face away and her shoulders were bowed. She was crying. 'Why have I done this to her?' I thought.

The tender moved fast. There was too much space between us. I looked around and there, moored in the sullen, rain-pocked river, sat the *Glengorm Castle*, like a reluctant duck.

She was an old ship of about 4,000 tons. The resentful smouldering in her bowels poured up through her funnel and would have obscured the sky, had it been visible.

But in the sunshine off the coast of Brittany she brightened up and wallowed her way across the Bay of Biscay like a retired whale enjoying its leisure. There were times when I thought she was overtaxing herself with her elderly gambols, but in the head seas of the Bay she always lifted her nose in time to take a good breath, and even in the steep Atlantic swell off the Cape she never rolled completely over.

For two of the three weeks of the voyage the sea was calm and life was a dream. For me it was a dream in rough weather too: I like the wilds of land or sea.

The voyage did not lack drama. Twin brothers of about my age shared the porthole cabin opposite mine. They were gay and good-looking and thoroughly merited the attention of the few pretty and unattached girls in the First Class accommodation to which we were confined. One of the brothers had particularly fine teeth but from about the middle of the voyage he was rarely seen, and when he was he seemed to be hurrying by on some urgent affair with his hand over his mouth. His brother, at the same time, had become uncommunicative and depressed.

There was much secret and puzzled speculation amongst the passengers, particularly the girls, over this strange reversal of the brothers' high spirits. It eventually transpired that one of them had awakened in the middle of the night, after a particularly Bacchic party, with a raging thirst. He had groped on the shelf above the wash basin for the water carafe and a glass, felt that the glass was half full and tossed the contents through the porthole. The glass contained not only water but a full set of dentures belonging to his brother who had, a year or two previously, suffered some disease of the gums which had necessitated the extraction of all his teeth.

Brotherly relations were strained. The continued pursuit of amour seemed quite impossible to the toothless twin and was decently refrained from by the other. At least that gave the rest of us a chance.

There was also the excitement of the Fancy Dress Night, when a husband on honeymoon, dressed as a policeman, accused another young man, robed in the habit of a monk, of lasciviously stroking his wife's legs, temptingly exposed beneath her fringed Robin Hood jerkin. The accusation, scarcely doubted by the rest of the male passengers who had had the legs under admiring but discreet observation, was hotly denied by the accused. Robin Hood burst into tears, which further incensed the husband. In the ensuing fight the monk was much hampered by his long habit and the policeman, appropriately, won. The opponents shook hands and Robin Hood was revived with champagne. All three became the best of friends and the party reached great heights; such heights that the husband suggested a swim before bed. It was, he said, a certain guarantee against hangover.

The swimming bath was a small wooden structure, five or six feet high, forward and just below the upper deck. From the edge of the upper deck hung a notice, often ignored by the bold of spirit: 'Diving Is Prohibited'. The top of the swimming bath wall was about two feet below the upper deck, giving a dive of about three feet into five feet of water. Any reasonably good diver could do it without hitting his head on the bottom.

The trio appeared in bathing costumes, tripping to the edge of the upper deck, led, as injustice would have it, by the now unfrocked monk, whose nose had stopped bleeding. All except the necessary lights of the ship were now out and the bath was in deep gloom. It was also empty.

The young man dived. There was a thud and then silence. The few of us that were watching realized what had happened and scrambled over the wooden wall and dragged out the body into the light, horrified. Its bloody appearance made it look much worse than it was. A good deal of skin was missing from the arms and face and chest, but nothing was broken, not even a tooth. The ship's doctor was called out of bed and dealt with the patient, efficiently, but without humour.

Three weeks at sea was too long for me and, despite the superb food and drink, the deck games and the interesting amour in which my cabin mate was engaged, for the last week of the voyage I was bored. There was too much sea in the Atlantic Ocean. I felt it ought to be punctuated with interesting islands, and in any case I was in a hurry to get on with the job of civilizing my noble savages.

The *Glengorm Castle* steamed into Table Bay on a fine Spring morning in the middle of October—such being the reversal of the seasons in the southern hemisphere. I have made a good many landfalls in many parts of the world since that day, but experienced none quite so lovely as that first sight of the Cape. Below the solid magnificence of cloud-topped Table Mountain and Lion's Head, winding down from the lower slopes of pine forest towards the sea, is a scattered garden city of gleaming white-walled and red-tiled houses, with spacious lawns and flower-gardens separating them. Even the port is clean and the centre of this city of wide streets does not crowd oppressively upon its people. I was unaware of the slums of non-whites. You only see those if you search for them.

The train journey of four days and three nights, from Cape Town to Livingstone, was a far better introduction to Africa than travellers by air get nowadays as they cover the thousand miles in a few hours.

The Flag-Wagger

The big Garratt engine never hurried, avoiding derailment as the narrow track wound through mountains, forests, deserts and swamps. It once demanded help, through the Hex River Mountains, and another engine was inspanned. Together they puffed through the mountains, stopping occasionally to drink a thousand or so gallons of water, until, with a farewell hoot, the assistant Garratt outspanned, and we ran easily across the desert of the Great Karroo, avoided the snowclad mountain ranges beyond it and pushed on to the High Plateau of Southern Africa, stopping more for coal and water than for stations, which were few.

I spent most of the daylight hours goggling through the window, observing the poverty of the few native villages, the ugliness of the sparse tin-roofed white settlements, the incredibility of the African sunrise and sunset, and the amazing moonscape scenery. I saw that deserts were not deserts, but bore flowers, shrubs and cacti that supported goats, ostriches and antelopes. I learned from my travelling companions, as we passed a green oasis, that a man could farm prosperously in the desert if he drilled for water and was lucky enough to find it at a couple of thousand feet before too many unsuccessful attempts broke him. I also discovered that I disliked heat, but that there were ways of minimizing it.

I was hot and restless the night we rattled towards Kimberley. By lowering the window and moving my pillow down the bunk a little, I could lie comfortably with my feet out of the window. This kept more than my feet cool for they acted as a scuttle, diverting part of the slipstream of the train right over the bunk.

Kimberley Station is busy and brightly lit. I suppose it was not surprising that I awoke to find somebody on the platform tickling the soles of my feet. It was a very attractive girl, surrounded by a little group of laughing admirers. I sat up and looked out of the window, grinning sheepishly.

'You're what I want for Christmas,' she said, astonishingly.

'I can't hold the train for two months,' I answered, 'I'd better get off.' But the Garratt hooted nastily and started to move towards open country once more.

On this journey I discovered space. This vast expanse of almost unpeopled land seemed endless and unfolded with detailed clarity in the dry transparent atmosphere. At night, under a moon and stars of improbable brilliance, the land itself brought close the reality of eternity. By day the emptiness of the country was puzzling. What was wrong with this land that it was so empty of people? It had a hard, cruel, beauty. It looked as though it had been baked and decorated, like pottery, but it was not fragile. A pickaxe would bounce off it and man could do nothing with it except perhaps in accidental soft spots here and there—faults in the pottery.

The few bridges that the train rattled across looked down on to boulder-strewn ravines littered with scattered pools. The waters would cascade down them in torrents when the rains came, wasted as they rushed hundreds of miles to the sea.

The kopjes, scattered isolated hills eroded by time into fantastic shapes, were surprising in their irrelevance. Only the distant mountain ranges, blue-hazed, looked inviting. If Northern Rhodesia was like this, my greatest difficulty in educating the natives would be to find any to educate.

During the third afternoon and night we ran on through Bechuanaland—the Kalahari desert—which also was practically empty but for cars and ox waggons at the sidings where we stopped and dusty earth roads twining away into nowhere, and white-washed police posts flying the Union Jack. Whom did they police?

Next morning the Garratt clattered on to the border post with Southern Rhodesia, and a Customs Office. The Customs Officer boarded us and came through the dining saloon at breakfast-time. He agreed instantly with everybody who said 'Nothing to declare' —as everybody did—and then sat down across the aisle from me and ordered coffee.

'Illicit diamond buyers, from Kimberley,' he said, 'they're the only people we're after.'

'How do you detect them?' I asked.

'We don't,' he replied, with a shrug, 'not unless we've had a tip-off. You can hide a few diamonds anywhere. And we can't give everybody castor oil.' Finishing his coffee, he returned to the Customs Office, and we pulled away into Rhodesia.

From now on there were increasing signs of life: cattle ranches, native villages, a straggle of houses and at last a tin-roofed bungalow city which the Garratt entered cautiously and with uneasy hesitations, like a country bumpkin approaching an escalator. This was Bulawayo, the last city I should see for two or three years. I had six hours to explore it in before catching another train to Northern Rhodesia.

The main streets were extravagantly wide, wide enough for a waggon with a full span of oxen to turn round in and the black people seemed more cheerful than those in Cape Town, where they had looked sullen or angry. The whites were gregariously genial and confident of voice. The shops were out of date with pictures or prints of Queen Victoria much in evidence on walls. In the town centre there was a large statue of Rhodes, looking suitably inscrutable.

I decided to buy a large and impressive revolver to go with my large and impressive terai hat. An obliging assistant in a gunsmith's shop thought a pistol would suit me better. He demonstrated the action of a Browning-type gun for me, and pointed out the safety catch. He put a magazine into the breech and showed me the automatic loading action. He then took the magazine out and waved the gun vaguely in my direction. I knew very little about guns at that time, but I believed that I had understood his explanation of the action of the pistol. If I had, there must be a cartridge left in the breech and the safety catch was off.

I suggested this, rather apologetically. The assistant was amused. 'I've been in this business for years,' he said, laughing as he pointed the gun upwards and pulled the trigger. The bullet made a neat hole in the ceiling. I decided not to buy a pistol or a revolver from him. He was most upset.

I wandered away from the gunshop towards the railway station, vaguely aware of unaccustomed things around me; a donkey cart, a large European matron in a sort of club chair on bicycle wheels being pushed by a black servant, a native woman hurrying across the street balancing a bottle on her head.

Life had suddenly become quite unreal. What was I doing here? If this was the Empire where was the glamour?

Back at the station the new train—and it was new, shining with newness—cheered me up. Trains were the best thing about Africa, I decided, and made for the saloon.

Northern Rhodesia, except for glimpses of the unbelievable Victoria Falls as the train crossed the bridge, looked very unimpressive at first sight—the first sight being of Livingstone, the then capital. Heat, dust, sunglare and corrugated iron roofs do not make an attractive combination.

I had been wondering what to wear for my first meeting with whatever Colonial Service officer—a high-ranking one, no doubt—would welcome me on the station platform. I had left Oxford in the era of wide and colourful Oxford bags, and equally wide and even more colourful plus fours. I unpacked both and eventually decided against a pair of mauve and white striped bags, in favour of a suit of plus fours in a very large black-and-white check. The plus fours had been my pride and, I thought, the pride of my college. They were certainly admired by my friends. Even the Sub-Rector had stopped me in the quad one day, with a look of wide-eyed interest, and asked, 'Where did you get that suit?'

I was met, not on the platform—there was no platform—by a clerk, John Nye, in a white open-necked shirt and shorts. He came straight towards me, through the other passengers, as if by instinct.

'You're Franklin,' he accused.

'Yes.'

'You're in the Great Northern Hotel,' he said. 'Let's get your baggage out of the van and I'll take you there.'

Followed by a trail of black porters, I walked along a red earth path, stamped out through yellow dead grass, to the Hotel. It was not a good hotel but at least it taught me to sniff surreptitiously at all fish or meat served in the tropics before eating it, and inured me to the bucket system. The buckets were housed, individually, in one-seater corrugated iron sentry boxes, each with its well-trodden path. Beside the bucket was a sandbox and scoop. Why these little constructions were called P.K.s I did not immediately discover. The only explanation I could think of at the time was that a pioneer builder, weak in spelling, referred to them in his plans as 'Privy Klosets'. I later discovered that the letters signify Piccanin Kaya (meaning Little House). They were occasionally adventurous places. One friend and colleague sat on one at a little-used rest house and rushed out protesting that he had been struck by a snake. Investigation revealed an indignant chicken hatching her eggs in the dry grass at the bottom of the bucket. She had pecked sharply upwards at the intruder.

My first night in the Great Northern Hotel was a restless one, but educative. As the sun set and the heat abated a little, I raised enough energy to visit the bar. I ordered a whisky, and had my first lesson in local custom. The barman silently pushed a glass and a bottle of whisky across the counter towards me. He returned to his stool in the corner and began idly shuffling a pack of cards. Perhaps it was the swinging half-doors through which I had entered and the barman's rolled-up shirt sleeves which brought to my mind memories of Wild West films and cowboys in saloons. The custom here was obviously the same—pour your own. Rather nervously and with an eye on the barman, I tipped up the bottle. The large tumbler was half full before I realized what had happened. The barman might look up at any moment. I panicked and said, 'I've taken rather a lot. What sort of a tot should I take?'

'You ought to know your own mixture, he replied. 'Take what you like.'

I filled the tumbler with water, drank it unusually quickly, feeling very small, and asked what I owed. The barman put a little card, printed at the top with the three letters 'I.O.U.', on the counter. 'A shilling' he said. Regarding my half-crown distastefully, he pushed it back to me. 'Write it down' he muttered, '. . . and your initials.'

Such was my introduction to the chitty system. In Northern Rhodesia it appeared one never paid cash for anything, just waited for a bill. A few years after my arrival the system was made illegal in bars as it was considered to encourage drunkenness.

My hotel room, a double, was littered with baggage; my own, unopened, and somebody else's, open and in disarray. After an inferior dinner, with an anti-malarial quinine tablet from the little bowl on the table as a savoury, I took a stroll through the town, stumbling occasionally in the dark on the rough sandy roads and stopping to investigate any combination of lights and noise—three bars and a small tin-roofed cinema. There seemed to be too many drunks in the bars and the film show was nearing its end, so I returned to the hotel and went to bed under the mosquito net. Livingstone, I decided, was certainly Wild West. So, I was to discover, was every white settlement in the Protectorate.

I went to sleep that night thinking that I did not like the Wild West, and was confirmed in this opinion when I was awakened by the shouting and cursing of a drunk who was pulling up my mosquito net. He eventually understood that the other bed was his and started to snore almost as soon as he had fallen into it. I awoke once more during the night to find him being sick. As far as I could see by the light filtering into the room from a naked electric bulb in the passage he was vomiting into an open suitcase. The morning revealed that the suitcase, happily, was one of his own.

CHAPTER THREE

The Inspector

After breakfast, in rather low spirits, I walked up the hill to the Department of Native Education. It consisted of a tin-roofed brick bungalow, divided into one large office and one small, with a verandah. It was staffed by the Director—whom I was to join—in the large office, an African clerk in the small office, and a Messenger whose name was Muliwani, on the verandah.

The Director was a courteous man, approaching forty, confirmed in the Church of England and the virtue of tennis. His task, he said, was to administer. The Messenger was for carrying messages; the clerk was for clerking and typing. 'And,' I said, humorously I thought, 'I am for Inspecting.'

For a moment he looked suspicious and annoyed. Then his expression changed to sadness and he said, 'They should not have sent you. I'm afraid you won't have much to do, but you can start by browsing amongst the files. We did not expect you for at least another year.'

I browsed until he took me to lunch at his house. We chatted amiably after lunch until he fell asleep in his chair. Some inner mechanism awakened him at five minutes to two, and we were back in the office punctually at two. Unpunctuality, I discovered, was a scarcely forgivable sin and rather caddish. You arrived at the office at 8 a.m. and 2 p.m. and left not a minute before noon, nor before 4 p.m. To arrive early and leave late, if you were overburdened with work, could be either praiseworthy or suspect as a method of attracting favourable notice and possible promotion, depending on the credibility of the overburden.

It was soon clear that I was not going to be overworked as The Inspector of Native Education in a Protectorate where there was hardly any education to inspect, only a few mission schools scattered over a sparsely populated country about four times the size of Britain. Nor was my inexperience likely to be unfavourably noticed. The Director, I discovered, was a seconded District Commissioner, an administrator, with no specialist knowledge of education at all.

In the next two or three months, the Director wrote letters for the clerk to type, while I checked expenditure vouchers, which were few, and wrote even fewer little minutes ordering the clerk's uniforms and stationery and other necessaries. The Messenger sold me some Barotse curios. In an attempt to fill in the remaining time, I wrote letters to my family and friends on important-looking departmental paper, enclosed in O.H.M.S. envelopes which I franked with a rubber stamp made especially for me with my name on it and sent to me, mysteriously, by the Postmaster General along the road, with a note saying 'Your franking authority is approved; herewith stamp.' Assuming it to be one of the perks of office and feeling that it would impress my friends and relations in England I made liberal use of it until John Nye, the clerk who had met me at the station, came cautiously into the office while my Director was out, to speak to me confidentially.

'You ought not to frank private letters you know, only official ones. The others should have stamps on. I thought I'd better tell you.'

'Why didn't the P.M.G. say so?' I replied.

'I expect he thought you would know,' said John gently. I felt guilty for weeks afterwards.

My Director departed on a three or four months' tour of the East African dependencies to study their native education systems, or perhaps to find out if they had any. I never saw him again. He left me in charge of the department, with one instruction. A Jeanes School, our very first Government School, was to be built at Mazabuka, some two hundred miles up the railway line. It could not be built without bricks and the Director of Public Works had promised that the bricks would be on the site by March 1st. I was to see that he kept his word. The D.P.W., nicknamed Paw Paw because of the florid complexion of his face, was a much harassed man of great ability, whom years of frustration had rendered choleric to an alarming degree. When the bricks' deadline was not met I rang him up and asked why. His reply was rude. A week later I tried again. His reply was abusive. I tried once more, and he was incoherent.

My duty was clear; *force majeure* must be applied. I asked John—now my friend and confidant—who was the working head of the Government, assuming that the Governor was King.

'The Chief Secretary,' he replied.

'Where is his office?'

'In the last tin shed across the road.'

I knocked on the door and entered. The Chief Secretary looked up, mildly surprised, and said, 'Hello, who are you?'

I told him and explained my duty in the matter of the bricks and my thwarted attempts to perform it. Without comment, he picked up the phone, demanded the D.P.W. and dressed him down in better selected and more effective terms than even Paw Paw himself could have dreamed of. He then put the phone down and said, 'You can't build a school without bricks, can you? They'll be there on Wednesday.'

He later became Governor of Mauritius and quite right too.

With my one duty accomplished, I seemed doomed to boredom in the office. But relief was close. I think John must have passed the word to the Secretary for Native Affairs, for whom he worked, that I had practically nothing to do. At any rate, the Secretary for Native Affairs asked me if I would like to help with some of his department's work, and I now spent some time collating statistics, sent in from the Districts, of the numbers of men, women, children, goats, cattle, sheep, pigs and so on, in the villages. Why these fascinating figures were wanted I neither knew nor asked. A numb apathy had overcome me during office hours.

Outside the office, life was interesting enough. The magnificent Victoria Falls were only about ten miles away and one could always get a lift on a goods train or borrow the office bicycle, which was quicker but sweatier.

I spent Christmas at the Falls, exploring when it was cool enough and lying in a cold bath, reading novels, when it was not. I also saw my first crocodiles and hippo, in the Zambesi river. I was assured that it was safe to swim in the river, and did so until a member of the Boat Club was eaten by a crocodile.

Unfortunately I could not afford to buy a car or even a motorbike and was at a disadvantage in the rush to the Falls Hotel when the urgent calls for manpower came from the Customs Post by the bridge. There was dancing every night at the hotel, and once the young Customs Officer and his immediate friends had ensured themselves of partners, the message would be flashed to Livingstone: 'Six American girls and a peach of a young widow from Johannesburg came in on the mail train this morning.'

The relief from boredom in the office appeared in the form of an Acting Director of Native Education, another seconded District Commissioner, a devout Catholic with no belief in the virtue of tennis but with, thank God, a sense of humour.

When I complained that I had no work to do, he said: 'An Inspector should inspect. You should go out on tour. I will make out an itinerary for you.'

I set out to inspect the only four schools of any size in the Southern Province, two of which actually took their pupils through two-thirds of the full primary course. The ordinary village schools of poles and grass or clay usually covered only the first two years of primary education and none covered more than the first four years. Many of their African teachers had not had more than four years of primary education plus a rudimentary teacher training course. They were paid about three pounds a month.

What the white missionary teachers of these schools which I endeavoured to inspect thought of me, I do not know. What I thought of their mission schools was that the Methodist one was devotedly run with skill, the Anglican school and the Catholic one were devotedly run with less skill, and the American mission seemed to be little more than a prosperous farm at which the schoolboys presumably learnt something about agriculture.

The Catholic school produced some adventure. I had detrained, with a few native carriers from Livingstone, at Magoye Siding, expecting to walk the five or ten miles to the Mission. I was delighted, as were my carriers, to find an ox waggon waiting for me, into which we piled the baggage and ourselves. The weather was fine, although the rainy season was well under way, and the ox waggon negotiated the drift across the Magoye River without much difficulty. Tropical rain then fell and continued to fall for most of the four days I was on the Mission station, inspecting both the boys' school and the girls' school and several other vaguely educational activities.

'You will never get back over the river' the Mission fathers warned. 'It will be in spate.' When I was ready to leave, I cycled out to inspect the river. It had trebled its width and, presumably, its depth and it looked as though the fathers were right. But the reputation of the Colonial Service was at stake! At all costs I must keep to my timetable.

'Could you possibly lend me two forty-four gallon drums, some planks and about a hundred yards of wire?' I asked the Father Superior. I explained my plan to him. 'I will make a raft to put my kit on, tie the wire to it, and swim across with it. If the raft and I part company, you can pull it back. I can look after myself. If all goes well the carriers can swim across after me. And if any of them can't swim they can hold on to the wire, which I'll make secure on the far bank.'

The Father Superior advised against it, but supplied the necessary equipment. All the fathers turned out to see the fun, including an enthusiastic lay brother who did most of the construction work on the raft. The nuns discreetly kept away.

I stripped and had enough sense to try the raft out without any baggage on it. As soon as it got out into the rush of the river, about three yards from the bank it was caught by the swirling current of the river, turned over and was hauled, with me, back to the shore. The raft was out.

'Let us' I said, 'tie the wire to the top of that tree. When I get across with it I'll tie the other end to the bottom of that tree on the other side. The wire will slope and it should be possible to slide the baggage down it piece by piece.' One of my carriers climbed the tree and tied the wire to it.

The lay brother scratched his beard thoughtfully and produced a ball of string from his pocket. 'Knotted,' he said, 'to the hundred yards of wire, this string might help you to get the wire to the other side. You can't swim straight across that current. You will land quite some way downstream if you land at all.'

He was right, but there was enough string, and I walked up the bank with it, drawing in the wire, to the appointed tree, secured the wire and stood, naked and proud, exchanging compliments with the fathers across the river. Unfortunately, I was standing on a nest of mpashi (red ants).

I had been so absorbed in the interest of the operation that I had not even thought of being eaten by crocodiles, let alone red ants, which I had never met before. An old African form of torture used to be to bury a man up to his neck in a red ants' nest until they had cleaned his bones.

The ants climb up your legs so lightly that they cannot be felt until their Commanding Officer gives the order to bite, when the assault company has reached your tenderest parts. They now reached mine and I jumped straight back into the river. After much ado, we eventually all got across the river with our kit and hitch-hiked a goods train.

I slept that night at a hotel strategically sited in the middle of an extensive European farming area. Dismounting from the goods train I made my way across the rails towards the lights.

A man was sitting at an iron table on the long verandah, alone, except for a bottle of whisky and a glass. Apart from him the place appeared deserted. I assumed, correctly, that this was the Manager, and asked if I could have a room. He looked up, annoyed at the interruption to his communion with the bottle, and said, 'How do I know? Ask my accountant—if he's sober. He's no good, that man. Damn it, one of us has got to keep sober, and I don't see why it should be me. I own the place.'

I found the accountant in his little office, sober but melancholy. He showed me to a room. After a passable dinner I sat on the verandah over a drink, listening to the shrieking of cicada beetles in the trees and observing, with some admiration, the decreasing level in the Manager's whisky bottle and his ability to stay on his chair.

Across the road, another goods train drew in from the south. Presently a woman, dressed as for the city, appeared within the light cast from the verandah, carrying a small suitcase which she put down on the edge of the road while she surveyed the verandah and the hotel's unimposing front, without enthusiasm. She was about thirty-five, and not unattractive. Her suitcase was shabby.

With an experienced eye, she decided that the man with the bottle must be the Manager, and addressed him nervously from the edge of the road.

'What do you want?' he said.

'I'm the new barmaid.'

'Barmaid!' he roared. 'Barmaid! What do I want with a barmaid?'

'But you engaged me,' she said, bewildered.

'Well go home then,' he replied illogically.

I sidled off to the accountant's office and suggested that something should be done.

The accountant said, 'I'll look after her,' and ran to catch up with the woman as she was walking back to the railway line. He led her circuitously back and found accommodation for her.

I awoke only once during the night, to find somebody shining a dim torch round my room. I yelled, 'Get out'. The intruder departed quickly and silently, and I got up and locked the door. I reported the attempted burglary to the accountant in the morning.

He smiled and said, 'It wouldn't be a burglar. Only somebody wanting a room. Anybody arriving late just looks into all the rooms until he finds an empty bed.'

It was an interesting tour. I made no attempt at real inspection of the schools. Even an experienced inspector would have been foolish to attempt that until he had studied the background to the system and of the missionaries who conducted it.

Each of the denominations—a Catholic bishop almost swore at me for calling his faith a denomination—had a brick bungalow primary school on the Mission station with about a hundred pupils. Within its sphere of influence scattered amongst the villages were a few dilapidated mud and thatch huts accommodating about twenty boys (some were almost men). They sat on the ground or on bush poles. They had slates but no books. The African teacher taught from his little book, printed in the local dialect. All the teaching was in that dialect except in the higher standards of the central primary schools where some English was taught. There were four different languages in the Province.

Many of the boys had no more schooling after their two years in the village school and quickly forgot (as I discovered later) what little they had learned. Others went on to the central school. If they were not within reasonable walking distance of it they became weekly boarders, bringing a bag of maize meal with them for food and trudging home at weekends.

There was no age grouping in the schools. A pupil might start in the village school at four or fourteen, the latter might get married while he was at the central school. There were practically no girl students. Girls were needed in the fields as cultivators, if the spectre of hunger was to be kept at a distance. At this time fathers did not want to be argued with by clever daughters: nagging wives were enough (and African wives are superb naggers). Mothers, concerned with finding suitable husbands for their daughters, did not want the girls to be put in the family way by the older schoolboys or even the schoolteacher, who had little enough to console him in his poverty-stricken drudgery.

The missionaries were evangelists, not educationalists, though a central school might have one or two properly trained white teachers. The missionaries' task was to save souls. A mounting roll of converts was, very rightly, their aim. The pagans needed the Bible so they must be taught to read it, at least in a vernacular translation. The Catholic mission even taught a little Latin so that the pupils could learn the responses. At both the Catholic school and the American school, run by Seventh Day Adventists, the Bible was 'education' and they taught practically nothing else.

The Methodist school was much more realistic, better equipped and staffed and clearly making a proper job of primary education. The missionary-in-charge was gently tolerant of me. We were walking along the passage between classrooms and a young man was sitting cross legged on the floor in the middle of it. As we navigated round him I asked, 'Who is he? Surely he should have the manners to stand up as we pass'.

The missionary smiled and said, 'That would be bad manners. Africa is rather topsy-turvy. The custom is to sit down before superiors. He's a school-leaver, waiting for his certificate.' I felt very small.

I remember nothing of the Anglican school except a priest in the excellent carpentry shop. He was a classical scholar from Oxford who, next to the Cross, adored carpentry and taught it well. All the missions taught a little carpentry and brickwork. They had to. They were starved of funds and they and the boys had to do all the maintenance and new construction on the station. The boys seldom finished the course. As soon as they thought they could earn money at the trade, they left and got jobs.

I returned to Livingstone feeling that I was beginning to understand Africa, and was invited to tea at Government House. I brashly told the Governor that we should never make a nation of Northern Rhodesia unless we educated its people. The missionaries should be left to their proper task of evangelization and we should create a system of free compulsory universal primary education, starting now.

'Where would we get the money?' he asked. 'Our annual revenue is a little over half a million a year.'

'From London . . . from the Government,' I said innocently.

He smiled cynically. I have never forgotten that smile. He knew what it took me years to realize, that British Governments would talk about their great civilizing mission in their overseas territories, but would not give the men engaged in that mission the money to do the job. Such small grants as it made to its colonies did not equal the actual cash that it gained from them in income tax from the United Kingdom-based companies engaged in commerce and industry in them, to say nothing of indirect economic benefits.

Soon after the tea party at the Governor's house, the Secretary for Native Affairs asked me if I would like to join the Administration as a Cadet. I said I thought I would, but wanted to think it over.

So I thought it over. I disliked Livingstone. Its Zambesi Valley climate was much too hot. It was a dull little tin-roofed town, with an aspidistra society which played bridge after dinner and invited you to tea or for a drink after you had dropped it your card on a little silver or brass plate on its verandah.

They were mostly nice people, these Government Headquarters officials. They sweated conscientiously in their shanty offices while their wives perspired genteelly at home, mourning the absence of their children who were being educated in England. Those of their daughters who had finished at school and returned to Livingstone were not exciting and there were only about half a dozen of them anyway.

I was bored; any clerk could do the paper work that I did in the office. My occasional tour to inspect a few mission schools was of no value to anybody and could not be until I had learned much more about Africa.

I was now twenty-three and had wasted the first eight months of my working life. That too was depressing. I wanted real, constructive, adventurous work for the Empire and some of its subjects. Perhaps I would find it in the Administration? I asked my Acting Director what Administrators did.

'In theory,' he answered, 'they rule the districts as District

Commissioners, under their Provincial Commissioners who are under the Governor who is under the British Government. But in practice, the District Commissioners rule their districts with little interference from above. The Administration is the cream of the service and you can finish up as a Governor. You'll get plenty of touring, village to village, on foot and bicycle.'

I thought it would be nice to be a Governor. I accordingly swore two oaths, one of allegiance to the King and the other to do my duty without fear or favour, and was sent to Serenje, 350 miles by train and a further 200 by a lorry which took nearly twelve hours to cover the distance, lurching about over an appalling earth road, its tyres throwing up billowing dust clouds. My pith helmet saved my skull from being cracked on the cab roof, but did my ears no good.

The journey was monotonous until just before the Serenje turnoff, when my transport rider (driver), Andrew Thatcher, jammed on the brakes, grabbed the rifle by his side, leaped out of the cab and shot a leopard out of a tree. It all seemed to be done in three seconds of fluid motion and I did not see the leopard until it fell into the knee-high grass below. The two lorry boys, one with an axe, jumped off the back of the truck as I got out to go and have a look at the kill, now invisible in the grass.

'Wait!' Andrew commanded sharply. We waited: there was no movement in the grass. Andrew went ahead with his finger on the trigger. 'It's dead,' he called.

We heaved the leopard on to the truck. It looked menacing, even in death. Andrew stroked it. 'It's a nice skin,' he said approvingly, 'a female, not too old, just right.'

The track narrowed to hardly more than the width of the lorry and the scenery changed. Before, there had been nothing but what Andrew called 'the bush', forest country of mostly spindly trees with their leaves turned on edge against the burn of the sun so that they gave little shade. Now we were in gently rolling country, grassland, patterned with forest strips at the higher levels. The grass was very short and green and the soil seemed to be black.

'Native hunters' Andrew explained. 'They burn the grass at this time of the year and the buck come out of the bush to graze on the new shoots.'

We passed several herds of antelope and some buffalo, silhouetted far from the road. The sun behind us was sinking fast. Everything glowed.

The track dipped and there was a great belt of reeds, gold-dusted at the tips, reaching far out towards a flash of water. It was very beautiful.

'Lake Moir,' Andrew said. 'See the geese flighting down? We'll reach Serenje in ten minutes, in those hills. It's a nice station. You'll like it.'

CHAPTER FOUR

The Admin istrator

SERENJE WAS A one man station until my arrival made it two—or, since I was a Cadet, perhaps one and a half. Backed with rocky hills where the klipspringer leapt from precarious boulder to impossible ledge on hooves as tiny as they were sure, the 'Boma' (District Headquarters) looked out from the edge of an escarpment, scanning what seemed to be (but was not) the biggest stretch of its ten thousand square miles of responsibility—a wide valley plain against a backcloth of tobacco smoke-coloured hills in which I later found implements of the Stone Age. The view was magnificent and I remained faithful to its beauty even after the comment of a visiting official from Livingstone to whom I pointed it out.

'What,' I asked proudly, 'do you think of that?'

He gave a straight reply. 'It looks to me like hundreds of miles of damn all.'

On my arrival at Serenje, I had no time to admire the view. It was nearly dusk, and I had to report to the District Commissioner. I found him walking towards the flagpole outside the office and introduced myself.

'We're just going to lower the flag,' he said.

A District Messenger, blue-putteed, red-fezzed, in a blue uniform with red facings, stamped to attention, turned smartly, wetted his lips and levelled his bugle. Three Airedales appeared and squatted in line abreast, waving their undocked tails enthusiastically and lifting their heads skywards. The District Commissioner stood to attention and I followed his example.

The bugler made a shaky start with the first note of the Last Post, but rallied as the Airedales joined in. They howled in ecstatic misery; they howled in chorus but not in harmony. From the depths of their souls they poured out all the pain and suffering of a dog's life, lingering on a last note of heart-broken despair, after the bugler had finished. They then got up and trotted off in tail-waving accord, as if mutually agreed that they had been in pretty good voice.

'Damn those dogs' said the D.C. and invited me to dinner. A month or two later he gave me one of the Airedales. It was the only dog I have ever known that ate oranges.

Tom Chicken, the District Commissioner, lent me a hurricane lamp after dinner, with which to find my way back to my euphemistic house. It was a small thatched oval building of two rooms, with a little front stoep, a bathroom and a store at the back, and another little stoep at the back on which stood a gauze contraption pretending to be a meat safe. Out at the back, some eight or nine paces away, was a kitchen and another twenty paces led one to the P.K. The roof of the house was full of sanitation-conscious rats who had made half-crown sized holes in the calico ceilings for their convenience. Some of the holes were over the bed and the thin, horsehair stuffed mattress had become stained and damp under repeated insult.

Hoping that the scurrying noises in the roof were made by rats alone and not by predatory snakes, I got under the mosquito net and waited for sleep, leaving a lighted candle by the bed in case something strange should happen. I was soon drowsy but, remembering the candle, I opened my eyes and saw two rats gnawing at its base. I blew it out and let them have the rest.

From somewhere close came a melancholy hoot. A little later there was a clumsy thumping and flapping of wings in the roof and much squeaking and scuffling. Splendid. An owl was preserving what I hoped would be a less than fair balance of nature.

That night the only sounds I heard from outside were the cries of a jackal and a hyena. At various times thereafter I was serenaded by almost every nocturnal creature under the moon—including lions. I used to get up and shut the window for lions, though they were never close, for the grunting or roaring of lions at night frightened me then, as now. Usually there is no need to fear a lion that makes a noise at night. In general maneaters operate silently, but there are exceptions to the rule.

Lions are exceptional beasts. Once some ate the Royal Mail. There was no road beyond Serenje, and mail for Petauke was dumped on us for forwarding by mail runners. Our mail runners were on the hundred-mile trek down the Luangwa Valley to

Petauke Boma, just before Christmas. Their mail bags were unusually bulky with hams, Christmas puddings and cakes and other gifts for the officials and missionaries of the Petauke District. The runners' path was contested by a small pride of lions and the men hurriedly dropped their bags and shinned up trees. The lions sniffed around the mail bags and must have got the scent of an over-ripe ham. They ripped the mail bags to pieces, scattering parcels and devouring, according to the mail runners, everything edible. I can believe that they tucked into Christmas puddings—for lions will eat almost anything when they are really hungry, but I still doubt if they swallowed the Petauke District Commissioner's socks, knitted for him by his mother. According to Henry, the Provincial Postmaster, in his reply to the D.C.'s complaint about the missing parcel, this is in fact what happened to the socks. There was some acrimonious correspondence on the subject, the final letter from the D.C. being addressed to 'Sock Stealing Henry, The Postmaster, Fort Jameson'.

I did not sleep well that first night and rose reluctantly to get to the office by eight.

Tom Chicken, already portly at thirty-five, explained my duties to me. 'The only one that matters, if you want promotion' he said, 'is tax collection. The more tax you collect the higher the Government will rate you.' This I discovered was a great exaggeration, but Tom was a confirmed cynic.

It seemed to me that the administration of the Protectorate must depend almost entirely on counting things and submitting the results to Headquarters in Monthly Returns. My duties were to keep the village census books up to date, not forgetting the goats and the tax entries; to count the Boma cattle, by sex and age; to count the prisoners, the bags of grain, the stores of all kinds and particularly the rifles and ammunition, the station labourers, Post Office stamps, court cases heard: anything animate or inanimate, abstract or concrete, that could be counted. I was also in charge of Weather. My first task every morning was to gaze knowingly at the sky, peer into the rain gauge, watch the drift of my cigarette smoke and record the results for Headquarters.

Tom, handing me the keys of the safe and a three inch thick ledger, introduced me to accounts. 'Everything you pay out' he said, 'you write on the left-hand page. Everything paid in goes on the right. At the end of the month you add up everything on the left and everything on the right. The difference between the totals—unless you break the bank, which you must never do—should come to the amount of cash in the safe.' I thought he had finished, but almost casually he added, 'It never does.'

'And does that matter?' I asked.

'Matter?' Tom exclaimed, shocked. 'It is the very foundation of the Empire! Fortunately it is not difficult to arrange. If the cash is short you pay in the balance out of your pocket. If there is a surplus you put it in that calico bag, known as the goat bag.'

I wondered what happened to the surplus eventually.

'We use it,' said Tom, 'on something sensible that they never give us enough money for, like roads. But do remember to take the goat bag out of the safe and hide it before the auditor comes. That's about once in two years, and it's a surprise visit—but there is a warning system.'

'How does it work?' I asked.

Tom grinned. 'Bush telegraph,' he said. 'You'll learn.'

And learn I did, under Tom's tuition. He was the best of teachers. His method was to throw me in and fish me out if the danger of my drowning became imminent, and then explain how I might have kept afloat.

In certain quarters, Tom acquired a reputation for being lazy. He was not, but he saw no point in doing anything that somebody else—such as myself—could do as well, and even less point in doing anything in conformity with an obviously futile instruction from headquarters which he judged—always correctly—would never be followed up. He was a great man but few people knew it, least of all himself.

His methods were sometimes unorthodox but always effective. He was highly intelligent, essentially human and a good artist. As D.C., Tom spent much of his day hearing cases at the Boma. Throughout one morning I heard the drone of witnesses coming from his office. He was trying a witchcraft case. At the end of it he came to my office, shaking his head.

'Very complicated case,' he said. 'You might be interested in having a look at the evidence.' On the indictment attached to it and a foolscap sheet there were a few scattered notes and drawings of an elephant with calf, a baboon, a bicycle and a silhouette of the interpreter. He then explained the case in clear detail, and his judgment, an acquittal, was as patently sound as usual.

As a Cadet, I had no judicial powers but sorted out complaints when Tom was away on tour, settling some off the cuff and leaving anything serious for his return. In Tom's absence one day, a villager, his wife and another man—a hunter—were brought into my office. In accordance with their custom they squatted on the floor and clapped greetings. The Clerk interpreted. The villager had agreed that his friend, the hunter, should spend a night with his wife in return for a hunk of meat. He was now demanding the meat, which had never been paid over.

I told the three of them, disgustedly, to go away. They went away as far as the compound, and awaited Tom's return. He gave judgment for the villager. I protested. He said, 'If you—Good Heavens, I know it could never happen—had engaged the services of a whore in Piccadilly, would you bilk her?' With that he strode angrily back into his own office.

Serenje, allegedly a township, consisted of two houses (the D.C.'s and mine), a native store, the Messengers' lines or compound, a gaol with one large communal cell and a guardroom, several tin roofed shacks for housing grain, tools and government stores, a tennis court, a five-hole golf course, and The Office, outside which was the flagstaff.

Every morning a small crowd gathered round this flagstaff, awaiting attention to their needs, which varied from postage stamps and sticking plaster to revenge or the protection of the law. In those days the area round the flagstaff was recognized in a very real way as a sanctuary. On one occasion a man who had killed another in a fight ran panting on to the green and flung himself down exhausted, with his arms round the flagstaff. His pursuers, close behind, armed with axes and spears, stopped at the edge of the green, foiled of their own justice and leaving the man to ours.

After a few weeks in the office, I was, Tom thought, fit to be let loose in the district.

'The Luangwa Valley' he said, handing me a sheet of cartridge paper with a sketch map of the area drawn on it. 'It hasn't been toured for two or three years.'

I commented that there did not seem to be much worth touring, judging by the small number of villages marked.

'There are more' he said. 'Map them in as you go, and do not camp in this area, particularly at Kachulu's village.' He ringed the village with a pencil.

I asked why not.

'There is sleeping sickness in the valley and it is very bad in that part. Wear long trousers, keep your sleeves rolled down and keep your fly-switch busy. If you get bitten by a tsetse fly that happens to be carrying the disease . . . well, there's no cure for it. There is an injection of some Bayer stuff—it's in the office somewhere—which is said to be a partial prophylactic, but I don't believe it and it makes you quite ill anyway.'

Death from a fly seemed quite improbable to me until, months later I repeated Tom's warning to a lay brother of a Catholic mission who was about to cross the valley. He was bitten by an infected fly and died. I was bitten by hundreds of them in the valley and elsewhere, over the years, but was lucky.

Tsetse flies did not worry me: the four District Messengers I was to take with me did. None of them could speak more than a few words of English.

'Can I take the Native Clerk with me?' I asked.

Tom looked at me, frowning, puzzled. 'What on earth for?'

'To interpret. I don't know the language.'

'You will when you come back,' said Tom, 'but I'll write you out a few key words, like "food" and "water", and "where is your tax receipt". Incidentally,' he added, 'the bridge over the Kaombe has been washed away. You can rebuild it when you get there.'

'But I don't know how to build a bridge.'

'It's easy,' said Tom. 'Any bloody fool can build a bridge.'

No further explanation was forthcoming. Instead he quickly ran through my touring duties and then said, 'What guns have you got?'

'Only a second-hand Westly Richards point four-two-five.'

'Go and get it. Let's have a look at it—and bring a cartridge.'

I brought the gun and he took out the breach bolt, squinted down the barrel and then tried the bullet in the muzzle and wiggled it from side to side.

'Hm' he said. 'They sold you a bit of a pup; the rifling is rather nickelled up and the barrel's a bit worn, but it will do; a .425 has got a hell of a punch. Use soft-nosed ammunition for everything except elephant and rhino. You'll spend less time following up a wounded animal then. And you must, repeat *must*, follow up anything you wound. Now listen.'

He quickly drew four very rough sketches of an indefinable beast, head on, rear on, broadside and three quarter facing. 'Until you're a crack shot—and never mind what you might have been on a range target, it's not the same—always go for the heart shot, if you can see it. You can get it from most angles. The heart is always just behind the shoulder one third up the body.' He then marked the heart shot and all the normal shots on the diagrams, giving a brief comment or two on each.

'You ought to have a shotgun' he said. 'Guinea fowl, partridge, duck . . . lovely eating. Good for hyena traps and so on, too.' Once more he sketched, two simple but effective shotgun traps.

'I've got a spare shot gun' he added. 'You can buy it if you like.' He looked at me long and thoughtfully and then murmured, as if to himself, 'I think you should have a revolver too. I've got an old army one somewhere. We'll see what state it is in.'

'Thanks,' I said, 'but I don't need it. I would never be able to hit anything with it anyway.'

Tom gave me a sort of far away look. 'The thing about a revolver is that you think you'll never need it,' he murmured. 'But if you've got it to hand when you do, you'll hit something with it then all right.'

I bought the revolver. In fact I never did use it, but on several occasions it was comforting to feel the bulk of it under my pillow—particularly at one time when I had a homicidal lunatic on my hands for a week in the bush.

I set off on a perfect morning—like all mornings in the dry season and most during the rains—at the head of a file of twenty-two carriers, four Messengers, a houseboy and a cook. There was music, as well as sunshine and the scent of flowering trees, in the air. I had left the packing to the cook and a quite unnecessary enamel chamber pot tied to the hasp of the metal 'office-box' jingled happily on the head of the carrier behind me, accompanied by the clashing cymbals of saucepans and frying pans in a tin bath further back. I joined in, ringing my bicycle bell for the sheer joy of it. The carriers suddenly burst into a song. I wish I could write the music, but these were the words of the first and all subsequent verses:

> 'Chingongo chaisa, chingongongo chaisa,
> Chingongongo, chingongo,
> Chingongongo, chingongongo,
> Chingongongo chaisa.'

Literally, 'chingongongo' means the big bell; 'chaisa' means comes. A free translation might be—'Listen to the mission church bell ringing; it sounds like this.'

And it did sound like that. The voices rang, cheerfully, confidently, as one song followed another. Most of them had verses, sung by the first man to start up, each verse being followed by the same chorus. Some were traditional, some were made up on the spot, and some were unfit for the ears of missionaries.

In the traditional songs was sometimes, it seemed to me, real poetry, though not perhaps in translation. One song the women sang went like this:

> 'You, young man! Do not stand there looking at me
> With the hot eyes of a sable bull,
> Burning desire into me,
> Enslaving my spirit.'

The impromptu songs sometimes commanded attention, as did any loud talking round the camp fire just after one had gone to bed. The words ranged from rank flattery to complaint, often a mixture of both, but their message was always clear. For example:

> 'The Bwana is a mighty hunter
> His gun is smeared with medicine
> He brings us meat.
> (*Chorus*) Ahyeeoh, Ayeeoh, he brings us meat.)
> The Bwana is a mighty hunter,
> He is brave and never misses. (Shockingly untrue)
> He brings us meat.
> (Chorus as before.)
> But for two days he has had sickness, (Also untrue)
> Perhaps his eyes, perhaps his legs.
> He's brought no meat.
> (*Chorus*) Ayeeoh, Ayeeoh, he's brought no meat.)

See now, today, he is much better,
His eyes are clear, and he will hunt.
He'll bring us meat.
(*Chorus*) Ayeeoh, Ayeeoh, he'll bring us meat.)'

Some songs were embarrassingly personal:

'Who is he who walks like a snake,
Swaying with his head poked forward,
Leaning forward and swaying
Like a snake in a jacket?'

'Can that be me?' I thought, straightening up and trying not to sway. 'Surely not!'

After a few miles, as we wound down the escarpment, the carriers' songs tailed off as they began to feel the heat of the day and the weight of their regulation forty-pound loads. The path was now too rough for cycling and I suddenly realized that I had neglected to take my compass sightings and speedometer readings whenever the path took a different direction. Comforted by Tom's comment ('It never comes out right anyway, but you can fix the point of return to meet the point of departure by adjusting backwards with your protractor when you draw the map'), I made a few notes by guesswork and resolved to keep my mind on the job. But resolution faded about a mile or two from the first village when I ran into the traditional welcome that I was to receive from so many villages over the years.

At the end of a tiring day, the dust and racket of this welcome could be wearisome. To have stopped it would have been exceedingly unkind. One grinned and waved and bore it.

The village children and the women, young and old, grandmothers and mothers with babies strapped to their backs, lined the path on either side, lululuing the praise call that is made by flicking the tongue from side to side between pouted, open lips while singing a long, high, even note. Then, bobbing, they clapped their greeting in slow rhythm. By this time I was abreast of them, and they trotted alongside, breaking into song as the carriers, refreshed by the thought of a night or at least a rest in the village, now nearly reached, quickened their stride.

There was a great sweating and scuffing up of dust. The carriers started up a song when the women stopped for breath and in between songs the carriers cracked bawdy jokes about the women. There were shrieks of laughter and more luluing, until we burst into the village in a scatter of dogs and chickens. Then, since it was the last village of the day, the camp was pitched close by, everybody lending a hand. The women, with superb carriage, brought clay pots of water balanced on their heads; the men, firewood and produce for sale; and the headman offered me a small present of a few bananas. I returned his welcome by giving him a present of salt.

They were long days, touring days, starting at dawn and ending with sunset, or later if the last march was misjudged or the litigation at the penultimate village droned on by the light of the fire. They were days that I loved then, and perhaps even more now in retrospect since mosquitoes and ticks and tsetse flies are no longer part of my life.

The work in the villages was simple.

One would run through the list of tax defaulters. 'Away on the mines' or 'Away on the railways' would be chorused as each name was read. Some of them were, and some were not and would be back in the village as soon as I left it. The occasional embarrassment after the chorus, caused by a man saying, 'I'm not on the mines and the book is wrong; here's my tax receipt' soon passed off.

Then there was a little lecture to be given on the virtue of having a village rubbish pit. The village headman would nod gravely. 'Yes yes, we will dig one tomorrow—or the day after.' That was the easiest answer. Occasionally one would get a little lecture back. One was from a minor chief and the subject was the desirability of pit latrines. 'The Government,' he said, 'is like a man with a new bicycle. For the first few weeks he polishes it, and oils it. Then he forgets and doesn't bother to oil it any more. We will dig these latrines. Nobody will use them, but it won't matter. When the Bwana comes round next year he will have forgotten about them. He will have another new bicycle.'

There is no reply you can make to the truth.

To become involved with international diplomacy on my first tour was, I think, unusual. Towards the end of the tour a runner arrived with my mail, which included a letter from Tom enclosing a printed circular signed by the Secretary of State for the Colonies and a cyclostyled one from the Chief Secretary in Livingstone. The former, which was verbose, explained that it had come to the notice of the American Consul-General in Johannesburg that large consignments of the United States flag, ordered by a wholesaler in that city, were being distributed to native stores in Northern Rhodesia and elsewhere, and were being bought by the women as 'limbo', lengths of brightly coloured cloth, to wear round the waist over the loincloth. (The torso was usually left bare.) The Consul-General had advised Washington of this insult to the flag, and a shocked American Foreign Secretary had instructed his Ambassador in London to lodge a formal protest with the British Foreign Minister, who had passed it on to the Colonial Secretary, who had passed it on to—amongst others—me. The instruction was that the practice of wearing the flag must be discouraged. The Chief Secretary's instructions were crisper. We were to stop the flags from being sold and to tell any women found wearing them to take them off and never to wear them again. No guidance was given as to where we might find legal authority for such action in the Laws of the Protectorate. Not that it seemed to matter, as there were no stores in the Valley, and I had seen no sign of the flag around anybody's bottom.

Two or three days later, as a village population was assembling for the usual 'indaba', I spotted the flag wrapped round a girl at the back of the crowd. I had acquired by this time a camp follower with a modicum of English learned from an American Watch Tower representative on the Copperbelt. I explained this business of the flag to him in a way that I thought the people might understand and asked him to pass it on to the Messenger, for delivery in the vernacular. I doubt if even the interpreter understood what I was talking about; certainly nobody else did.

The Messenger's version was roughly this: 'All the white men's countries are ruled by Kings. Each King has a flaggy, a piece of cloth on a pole like the one at the Boma, only they have different colours. The flaggy is the King's special charm which gives him great strength. It must not be used by other Kings and it must stay at the top of a pole. Now the American king has found out that women here are wearing his flag and he has complained to the English king who has complained to the Bwana and said that women must not wear this flag.'

There was a baffled silence. I went into conference with the interpreter who told me, in English, the Messenger's version. We had another go, but it was hopeless.

Finally I said, 'Tell that girl she must take that cloth off.' They understood that.

The girl was about fourteen, tall and with the perfect carriage of her race. Her breasts were beautifully rounded. She rose gracefully to her feet, swiftly whipped the Stars and Stripes from her waist and stood holding it between her finger and thumb at arms length, almost in the pose of a strip-tease dancer at the finale. She then let it drop and stood gazing at me. She was not wearing a loin-cloth.

All heads were turned towards her, and there was silence. I damned the American Consul-General, and said, weakly, 'Tell her to put the cloth on again.' From then on I disregarded the instructions.

I got through the indaba with lowered eyes. Even my Messengers, I thought, must think me a queer fellow. I discovered later that they did, but not for the reason I had thought. And what would the villagers think of me?

I sat outside my tent after dinner, brooding over the incident and heard the slow clapping of someone wishing to attract attention. It seemed to come from under a fig tree outside the range of light from the fire. I thought if I ignored it, it might go away. It did not, so I shouted for a Messenger.

'Who is that clapping over there and what does he want?' I asked.

'I don't know' he said, but I thought he looked rather shifty.

'Well, go and find out.'

'It's that girl' he said on his return.

I was worried. I thought she was going to complain about being given an indecent order. 'What does she want?' I asked.

'Nothing,' said the Messenger, and the shiftiness was plain.

'Come on,' I said. 'You know what she wants. What is it?'

'Don't you want her?' he asked.

'No' I said, baffled. 'Why should I?'

'Well,' he answered, 'why did you want to see her with her cloth off?'

I told him to tell the girl to go away, which he did, reluctantly. I sat thinking about it all and about the lightish coloured girl that

I'd seen hanging around my garden at the Boma several times, and another, very black, that had done the same later on. I remembered the well-meant advice of a senior official in Livingstone with whom I had dined just before I left for Serenje. 'Don't worry,' he had said, 'if you have a black girl. You're sure to, but don't let it get on your conscience. Everybody does it. You'll be lonely. It's natural.'

I never did have a black girl, at Serenje or anywhere else, partly because I never saw one that seemed sufficiently attractive; partly because I couldn't imagine what I would do with the girl or say to her, outside the bedroom; and partly because I thought it would be letting down the Service. On the last point I was hopelessly wrong. As I was to discover, any bachelor official or grass widower who did not take on a native girl was regarded as queer by the people. He had the *droit de seigneur* of a chief, and there could only be one (unflattering) reason why he did not exercise it.

Loneliness was the curse of outstations. It led occasionally to suicide or, rarely, to drugs (morphine usually) or drink, but more often to harmless eccentricities. There was one District Commissioner who used to lock himself in his house on the rare occasions when a white man visited his station, and was either successfully coaxed into sociability or stayed locked in until the visitor left.

I once listened to a missionary on an isolated station for nearly an hour, trying to find out what was troubling him. Nothing he said made sense except the constant repetition of the remark 'The situation is quite impossible. It cannot possibly go on.' I could not get out of him what the situation was, though he seemed to think that he had explained it over and over again. He needed leave and was given it soon afterwards. Perhaps he was saner than I thought. On one occasion when I particularly wanted my leave early to fit in with the English summer and could not get it, a colleague advised me to 'Drive into Provincial Headquarters and walk around their offices with no trousers on.'

Although there were times when I would pace up and down my little verandah at Serenje talking to myself, I kept reasonably sane. Work, studying law and native languages (there were examinations which had to be passed) were a great help. I was more fortunate than some. There was an Australian white hunter living only twelve miles away, and a mission station about twenty miles off, on a path suitable for cycling, so I had neighbours. But you just had to learn to live with loneliness on outstations, for, despite the fact that, whether at the Boma or on tour, you were surrounded by people, you were always alone; alone with a load of responsibility.

You were judge, marriage counsellor, policeman, tax man, doctor—everything. It was to you alone that the people brought their more serious problems and complaints, and yet you were not one of them. You were a man apart. They made you that. If they had not, you would have made yourself that, of necessity. You could not have ruled otherwise, and you had to rule. You listened to the people's troubles; you could not confide in them your own worries, which were often concerned with your inability to deal adequately with theirs.

There were unhappy periods, especially during the rainy season when the weekly mail lorry could not get through for a month and it was impossible to cycle to the mission on a Sunday. Tom and I kept to the wise tradition of outstations and did not see much of each other outside the office. Two men, isolated, insulated from their world by a world not theirs, a primitive world, can easily come to hate the sight of each other.

More than once, I thought, 'You're young and you're mad to stay here. You were a scholar. What is there here to stretch your mind? You were gay, one of the boys where the bright lights flashed and girls waved from cars and bands played on the dance floors. Go back. Go back where you belong.' Perhaps if I had had the money to get back I would have gone, but I'm glad I did not. It took a long time for Africa to grow on me; when it did it took deep root.

CHAPTER FIVE

Hunting

THE REPUTATION I acquired as a successful hunter and meat-provider helped to make up for my shortcomings in other directions. The things the people valued were simple, and good shooting and a full belly were two of them. Their tolerance and forgiveness were sublime.

On one occasion I had given a man a rather virulent ticking off. I saw him the next day looking, as I thought, rather morbid. I asked if he was brooding over the previous day.

He looked at me, surprised, and then smiled.

'I am not a woman, to bear a grudge,' he said.

A reedbuck and a leopard were responsible for my exaggerated reputation as a hunter. After a weary and fruitless afternoon, when it was dusk a reedbuck broke out from the edge of the forest some way ahead and ran across a wide dambo, then turned and ran parallel to the other side. I could just follow it with my eyes until it ran in front of a small, conical anthill, when I lost it. I put that down to the bad light and yet, I thought, I should have seen it after it passed the anthill. There was just a chance, the anthill being fawny brown in colour, that the buck, with its perfect knowledge of camouflage, had stopped in front of the anthill to look around and see if it was being chased.

There is a temptation, which should be resisted, to take a most unlikely shot at something after walking ten miles or more and seeing nothing. The distance to the anthill was difficult to guess and the reedbuck was probably not there anyway. If it was, I thought 500 yards might be something like the range. But why bother about putting up a leaf sight? I would just take a pot shot at the top of the anthill pinnacle and see what happened. I fired, and saw the reed-buck leap away from the anthill with that extra impetus that often follows a heart shot. After the leap I could not see it.

Amon, my cook, and the Messenger I had with me had not seen

the buck from the start and were looking at me, baffled.

'Let's go and collect it' I said.

'Collect what?' said Amon.

'The reedbuck.'

'That wasn't a reedbuck you fired at. It's an anthill.'

When we reached the buck we found it dead, shot right through the heart. It was a fluke in a million but it was no use trying to tell Amon that, not that I wanted to.

The leopard had been taking dogs from the Messengers' compound at night. This is always potentially dangerous as the beast may go on to seize a child. Traps were set, with no result, and the Messengers' own efforts to hunt the beast down were not successful. Very early one morning an aggrieved Messenger, whose dog had just been seized, knocked me up and asked me to go after the leopard. He came with me to help me to track the leopard, and I took my dog Hamlet. The spoor was easy enough on the sandy earth of the Boma at Mpika, but once we got into the rocky hills where we found the remains of the dog, the catlike pads of the leopard left no mark. But Hamlet was straining at the leash and was obviously, I thought, on the scent.

We scrambled through the hills and caught a glimpse of the leopard moving off at the same time as we heard a troupe of baboons barking furiously. What was really happening, though I did not realize it at the time, was that the leopard was following the baboons. He would have kept close to the troupe, hoping to pick off a straggler for his next meal. No leopard would dare to attack baboons marshalled ready for him, or even put himself in a position where they could encircle and attack him.

He changed his plans when he saw us and made for the rockiest part of the hills. The going was tough and we could not keep up with him, so I slipped Hamlet's leash, hoping the dog would bay him until I could catch up. Hamlet, it seemed, had other ideas and shot off after the barking baboons.

Running and scrambling over boulders and fissures, I followed the course I thought the leopard had taken and left the Messenger far behind. Sweat was running into my eyes, the foresight of my rifle hit a rock and I had had about all I could take when I suddenly saw the leopard on top of a huge boulder about twenty yards up the hill. He was facing me three-quarters on, with one forepaw raised as if to strike and snarling at me viciously. He was ready to attack but warning me off first.

I tried to steady the rifle against a tree, but I was blown and panting and the foresight was going round in small circles. Also I saw that the ivory tip of the foresight had gone and I wondered fleetingly if the foresight had been knocked out of true. But (and this for a hunter is the height of stupidity) I had lost my temper with the leopard. So I pressed the trigger at what I hoped was the bottom of the circle the foresight was making. The bullet raked him right through and he fell off the boulder, dead. Later, I found that the foresight was bent and I had to get a new one. It was a lucky shot.

The Messenger came up in a few minutes and did a brief little song and dance act which I thought very odd. Then we cut a pole and strung the leopard on it and went back to the Boma. On the last stretch of the hills, approaching the cleared land of the Boma, the Messenger started bawling out a song, and as we reached level ground the entire compound, men, women and children, were around us, screeching the song with him.

I learned more about leopards later. They attack like a hard-driven tennis ball, fast and bounding, and if I had wounded this one I would have had a difficult time but perhaps not a fatal one. One of my friends, a doctor, lost an arm, and another spent some time in hospital through an encounter with a leopard. In both cases the leopard was badly wounded. I doubt if any man could fight an unwounded leopard and win; he would certainly have no chance with a lion. The Baila, the best fighting and hunting tribe in the Protectorate, rated them both equally dangerous with man. If you had killed a lion, a leopard, or a man, you were entitled to wear a red feather in your hair.

Man-eating lions are, of course, in a class of their own. They were usually not, as is popularly believed, old or injured lions incapable of pursuing and killing their normal prey, but lions driven by hunger in areas where game was very sparse. The man-eater would enter a village after dark and seize a dog or a goat. From this he would graduate to a child or an old woman and, once having lost his fear of humans, would attack anyone, though rarely in daylight.

Nothing terrorized the villagers more than a man-eater, which they invariably believed carried the revengeful spirit of an ancestor whom they had somehow offended, perhaps in some accidental impropriety in the performance of his funeral rites.

'Namweleu', killed eventually by a District Commissioner friend, James Lemon, from a tree, was the worst man-eater I ever heard of. My attempt, from 500 miles away, to help to destroy Namweleu was quite ineffective. I heard from James of the appalling depredations of this lion and the great reluctance of village hunters to go after it, since it was bewitched and therefore impossible to kill. I was at this time in the new capital, Lusaka, and of sufficient seniority to exercise a little influence. The reward for killing a lion which was classed as vermin—much more appropriate than 'King of Beasts'—was £5. Namweleu had already eaten about twenty people. I thought if the reward were put up to £100 the local villagers might be more inclined to go after him. The Chief Secretary decided to make it £10, pointing out in his minute that this must not be regarded as a precedent. It was certainly not regarded as any encouragement by the villagers.

A lioness operating with Namweleu was killed before the death toll had risen very high. A village teacher met her on a path and stood still, hoping she would move off into the bush, but she charged. The teacher, who was carrying two short stabbing spears drove one home as she leapt and fought her until he managed to drive the other spear through her lungs. She staggered off to die. The teacher, terribly mauled, lived for two days.

But Namweleu, roaming over a territory of several hundred square miles, led a charmed life.

Bands of District Messengers scoured the area. Namweleu seemed to know where they were and killed somewhere else. Traps and poison failed. He broke into huts to seize his prey, sprang on a teacher riding a bicycle, caught an old woman coming out of church, attacked small parties, circling and feinting before the final charge on the individual he had selected. The only man that got under his skin was a villager who calmly heated his spear in the fire while Namweleu was scrabbling on the hut roof trying to get in, and then drove the spear up through the thatch.

The people of the area were completely terrified. None would venture out, by day or by night. Normal life came to a standstill. Something had to be done. It was up to the Boma. James Lemon, accompanied for some time by a government doctor, set out after

Namweleu. For weeks they camped, each sleeping at night on a tree platform at whatever village each fancied Namweleu would visit next.

One night the doctor and James, at neighbouring villages, had each set up a dummy near a fire. Namweleu visited the doctor first. He switched on his torch and pulled the trigger as Namweleu shook the dummy, but in the excitement he forgot to push the safety catch off and Namweleu was moving fast before he fired and missed.

James was outwitted. Namweleu approached roaring, announcing his presence, and James levelled his gun. There was a minute of silence. Namweleu crept round to the side of the clearing and suddenly streaked past the fire from an unexpected direction snatching the dummy in his stride. James's shot missed.

The doctor eventually had to return to his patients. James plodded on, covering over two hundred miles in two weeks, at the end of which he received and ignored an order to return to his station immediately. He would think up some excuse later. In the event, none was needed: for nothing succeeds like success.

The night before, Namweleu had seized a woman from a village and dragged her to a dense mushitu by a stream. The husband, crazed with grief, collected his spears and made towards the grunts that revealed where the beast was feeding. In pitch darkness he had no chance. He was killed within three paces of his wife's body.

The next night James, having tied the body of the dead man to a tree and himself sitting up another, kept his shotgun trained on the body, listening to every rustle of grass, every little noise in the forest. Alerted by the snap of a rotten branch, he waited, trembling with excitement, until he heard Namweleu snarling with rage at being unable to drag the body from the tree. James switched on his torch. Namweleu, half up on his hind legs astride the body, had started to eat it on the spot. He turned his head, teeth bared, eyes glaring red into the beam of light. Concentrated shot from the choke barrel hit him behind the shoulder. He reeled about drunkenly, coughing blood, and was staggering into the long grass as the second barrel load caught him over the heart.

It was two days before James could start back for the Boma. He was carried on the shoulders of the tribal headmen from village to village, led by the local Chief and his blind musician, surrounded by a singing, dancing, drumming crowd, bent old women, toddling children, the entire population.

Within the stockade of the Paramount Chief, James, daubed with maize meal and anointed with beer, sat cross-legged while the Paramount tied a bunch of red and white cock feathers to his hair and the people shouted assent to his election as a prince of the Bemba royal family.

There is perhaps a touch of schizophrenia in most people, which may account for the fact that many hunters are wild animal lovers and will take endless trouble to set the wing of an injured bird or nurse some lost baby animal to maturity. Some of these wild things can become fascinating and affectionate pets but, if allowed their freedom, and they must be allowed it, will almost always disappear when they are ready to mate, never to return.

The most amusing pet I ever had was a bushpig or wild boar. I brought her up on the bottle and she had a fondness for it ever after. The curious thing was that she went off milk. She alone, of all animals in my experience, had a weakness for alcohol. She had a preference for gin, but anything going would do. Whenever I had a party in the garden she would lap up every unwatched drink put down on the grass. She never got drunk, only obstinate. She could not be driven away. She would stand immovable and stubborn, and if you picked her up and carried her off—she was a hefty load—she would scream abuse until you put her down, and then return smartly to the party.

Her name was just 'Pig' and, apart from her beautiful brown eyes, long black eyelashes and small black shiny hooves, she was no showgirl. She was a solid barrel of mischief and affection. She would chase anybody that was obviously afraid of her (she looked a bit fearsome) until the pursued climbed a tree, tripped, or could run no further. She would then stand looking at him for a moment with a twinkle in her eyes, and move off to some other small adventure.

I managed to discipline her sufficiently to keep her out of my bed and my bath, but visitors found her rather difficult. I once lent my guest cottage to a honeymoon couple, friends of mine and of Pig's. There was a double bed in the bedroom and a divan in the sitting room.

One night there was a row between the couple and the indignant bride left the bed and went off to sleep on the divan.

The husband awoke in the morning with that sense of gloom and doom that husbands have after such rows. This was the end, the terrible end of love, of life itself. The things he had said. She would never forgive him.

But . . . what was this? A warm body stirring beside him; soft moist lips on the back of his neck. Thank heaven! All was right with the world. He turned over and looked into the fond brown eyes of Pig. He called to his wife, and the subsequent hilarity healed the breach.

Every afternoon, when I came back from the office Pig would run up to me and wait to be scratched. As I scratched her rough, hairy side with a stick or a stone, her eyelids would flutter and close. Then she would keel over and collapse in a swoon. When I stopped scratching she would take some time to come round and flutter her eyelashes at me, asking for more.

Then we would walk across my little valley into the hills. Pig, following respectfully behind, stopping occasionally to rootle up some delicacy from the hard earth with her soft but remarkably tough snout, was as obedient as a dog until she thought I had forgotten about her. Then she would suddenly dart between my legs, gauging my stride just right, and twisting her body in order to bring me down. As I lay there on the ground she would stand listening interestedly to my language.

She went off one day and never came back. I hope she found a mate and had dozens of babies. But the forest is dangerous for pigs.

CHAPTER SIX

The Amateur Doctor

IF MY HUNTING provided valuable protein for a few, my amateur doctoring gave a little help to the health of even fewer. Even with every outstation administrator throughout the British Empire doing the same, the percentage of people that could be helped was microscopical. Medical services were what the people needed and appreciated more than anything else. Yet these services were provided almost exclusively in the towns, and there most inadequately. In the vast rural areas they were practically non-existent, except at a few mission stations.

There was no money for expanding the medical services. This was effectively brought home to me at Serenje, when a Messenger came to me one night having just been bitten on the heel by a puff adder. I had bought myself an anti-snake-bite outfit in Cape Town when I got off the ship. It contained only one phial of anti-venom serum, which was quite expensive stuff. I injected it into the Messenger's leg and he was soon all right.

I was on a Cadet's pay, thought the Government Medical Department should replace the serum and wrote to the Director of Medical Services accordingly. He sent the replacement but wrote that anti-venom serum must never be used on natives as it was very expensive and his department could not afford to pay for its widespread use. Money was needed. The local government could not, and the British Government would not, provide it.

Paradoxically, the native peoples of the territories were also partly responsible for the slow progress of medical services in the form of hospitals. If you went to hospital you either died or came out minus a leg or an arm or something else. Very few patients would agree to go into hospital, even if there was one within a reasonable distance.

They would go eagerly enough to a doctor of one kind or another; to the village medicine man for charms or herbs, or to the witchdoctor for the removal of the spell or the evil spirit that was causing the pain in the belly. They would also, hoping for the best of both worlds, go to a white doctor, either before or after treatment from their own expert, or even simultaneously. They would go to the white man they knew, who lived among them, and they were not interested in his qualifications. When I told them that I was not a doctor, that I had no medicine for this or that, or that I did not know what was wrong with them, they would sometimes grumble and say that I just did not want to be bothered with them.

At Serenje, among the crowd outside the office or the touring tent there would usually be somebody wanting medical attention. The medical stores were on a shelf in my office—simple drugs, disinfectants, bandages and so on. There was a Medical Orderly called Moses. What training he had received, if any, I never discovered, but he was good at cleaning and bandaging wounds. For sickness of any kind he used the same remedy: pink boracic lint soaked in hot water.

He came to me one day holding a thermometer and said, 'The Second Messenger is very sick. His temperature is 120.'

I said, 'It can't be, he'd be dead before it rose that high.'

I looked at the thermometer, which registered 102, and said, 'What do you think is wrong with him? Malaria?'

'I think so, Bwana.'

'What have you given him?'

'I have wrapped hot pink lint round his belly, Bwana,' said Moses.

Amateur doctoring was one of my happiest little sidelines. It was certainly more appreciated by the people than some of my other activities. With our medical stores was a little booklet compiled by Burroughs & Wellcome, giving a list of diseases and ailments with their symptoms and treatment, if any. Against some diseases such as sleeping sickness (for which there is now a cure if it is taken early enough) there was the ominous note 'Fatal. No cure.'

I did my best and often did not know with what result, because the patient would wander off back to his village, anything up to a hundred miles away. One man was brought to me with his eye hanging over his cheek bone. I washed out the socket with a boracic solution, pushed the eye back and bandaged it with pink lint. I heard later that this saved his eye, but I never really knew.

Some faith healing was achieved with things like potassium permanganate solution because of its attractive colour, and with kidney pills which produced a bright green urine. My personal speciality was to give any particularly miserable patient a drink of Eno's Fruit Salts from my private stock. Cold water that boiled and bubbled obviously had magical properties.

I think I cured an old woman brought in one evening on a litter, in the crisis of pneumonia, by giving her a slight overdose of chlorodyne, hoping that the morphia would help her to sleep. She certainly had a good night's sleep and recovered and came to thank me for curing her.

I never enjoyed bandaging up lepers, partly because it was messy but mainly because I was, stupidly, scared. My incorrect knowledge of leprosy was based on the bell-ringing lepers of The Bible and, until a doctor enlightened me, I thought it was terribly contagious.

On the medical shelf there was a bottle of champagne and a bottle of brandy, listed as medical comforts. The champagne was supposed to help blackwater fever patients to pull through, but any prospector, hunter, or missionary, who developed blackwater while wandering about the district had either to recover without it, or be lucky enough to be within carrying distance of the Boma.

It can be worrying being even moderately ill in a strange country of strange diseases, hundreds of miles from anywhere. Tom Chicken taught me a valuable lesson about this on one of my early tours in the district. I had, I think, some sort of flu, or perhaps a mild attack of malaria. Whatever it was, I could tell that my temperature was up. I felt rather groggy and lay in my tent for a day or two, damning Burroughs & Wellcome for not packing thermometers in their travelling boxes, and worrying about which of the incurable tropical diseases I might be developing. I was only about two days' march from the Boma and sent a runner in to Tom with a letter giving him some general news, and at the end asking him casually—there must be no discernible unstiffening of the British upper lip—to send me a thermometer. The runner returned without one and there was no reference to it in Tom's reply. By this time I was feeling fine and getting on with the tour. I assumed he had forgotten the thermometer and made some reference to it when I returned to the Boma.

'Don't blame Burroughs & Wellcome' he said. 'I took the thermometer out of the box long ago and I didn't send it to you because there is nothing so likely to make a man lying up in the bush panic and get worse than taking his temperature every five minutes and watching it go up. The great thing is not to worry.'

One item of medical knowledge I drew from Tennyson. Serenje, at about 6000 feet, was reasonably cool and at night it could be bitterly cold. On one such night I was awakened by my servant with the interesting news that there was a dead man outside. From the loud arguments going on at the back of the house, there were obviously others that were not dead. I went out and found four men, bare to the waist and carrying spears. Their bundles were lying on the ground beside a long pole to which a blanket was strung. The blanket, it seemed, was shrouding the corpse. The District Messenger whom the party had first contacted was questioning the men. 'They say it was an accident, Bwana' he said.

I pulled the blanket aside and the corpse looked at me with a pained expression and sat up. There was a split in his stomach about two and a half inches wide, the width of a spear blade.

'Accident?' I thought. 'Take me for a new boy, do they? I'll show them.' 'Out with it!' I said sharply. 'Who did it?'

Their story was that they were on a long trek, carrying their heavy bundles on their heads. The wounded man had tripped, thrust the haft of his spear into the ground to steady himself and had fallen on the blade. I began to believe them when I examined the wound, which went straight upwards under the layers of skin and muscle; how far up I could not tell.

By this time we were all shivering with cold and I had bandaged the wound. Somehow, into my mind came a line from *Mort D' Arthur*: 'I fear my wound hath taken cold and I shall die.' The man's one blanket was clearly not enough to keep him warm, so I gave him two of mine. The wound healed in a week or two and the party continued their journey. I told my servant to boil the two blankets in a solution of a disinfectant we called 'dip'. He only washed them with soap, I later discovered, and louse eggs had been laid in them. The weather had become colder and I was glad to have the blankets back on my bed, until one night I awoke itching all over my body. An inspection by lamplight revealed nothing, but in the morning sunlight I discovered I was lousy. By eight o'clock I had still not finished delousing myself and the bed, and I sent a note to Tom explaining why I would be a little late at the office.

A note came back which seemed to me to suggest an unworthy suspicion: it said 'Send specimen of lice'. I put one in an envelope and sent it to the office, which I reached quite soon afterwards myself. Tom and the Head Messenger were crawling around the floor on their knees. Tom looked up and said, 'I dropped the damn thing; help me find it.'

I grew fond of the black enamelled tin box labelled 'Burroughs & Wellcome', that bobbed along on somebody's head behind me whenever I went on tour. For lesser ills its cough mixture and liver pills and disinfectants and eyewashes and the rest did have some real curative effect. Cough mixture and chlorodyne, being sweet and warming, were always in demand and I am sure that a certain amount of both went down the throats of healthy but persuasive liars.

As soon as I camped, the sick from the surrounding villages would start to arrive. Some, believing that they were bewitched and therefore doomed to death, would hold back. So would those with a venereal disease, for whom (as for so many others) I could do nothing anyway. Penicillin, the sulpha drugs and other miracle workers had not then been discovered; when they did come into use, venereal patients swarmed around the new medical travelling vans.

Sometimes I would be taken to the hut of a very seriously ill person. If possible I had the patient carried outside into the sunlight, partly because inside it was too dark to see and partly because in the foul atmosphere of the hut I was afraid of catching whatever the patient had got.

A leper would have to crawl up to the camp by himself from his isolated hovel of branches and leaves in the bush. Nobody would touch him. I would put a useless bandage onto what was left of a foot or a hand, because I thought it made the man feel that he was somebody after all and not just an object. Even to see and talk to the strange white man was, I thought (and I know I was right) a brief distraction from his desperate unhappiness and gave him something to think about afterwards.

This sort of work may not have helped the sick very much but it at least helped to prevent me from becoming an automaton administrator, doling out justice and orders to cyphers that I had forgotten were human. This was always a temptation; to rule the people with cold logic and by rigid ethical principles.

The problem of what to do with seriously ill people was a depressing one. For the living skeletons with sleeping sickness and for the advanced lepers nothing could be done. But there were people with terrible wounds, or with diseases that I could recognise and who would obviously die without proper medical attention and nursing.

Would the patient survive being carried on a litter of poles and bark rope for up to a week to the Boma, there to await a lorry which would bump him for at least one day down the Great North Road to the nearest doctor and hospital at Broken Hill?

You looked at the map of the area which you yourself had made. If the carrying party kept as far as possible to the inter-village paths running west it would cut into the road fifty miles south of the Boma and that much nearer Broken Hill. It was the height of the dry season so the carriers should be able to ford the streams easily and there would be at least one lorry a day and no bridges swept away on the road.

You looked at the patient's leg, terribly mauled by a crocodile and by now stinking and gangrenous. You judged, God help you, that he would survive the journey, that amputation might save his life and that he would certainly die without it.

You explained this to him and asked him if he would agree to be taken to hospital. He replied emphatically, 'No'. You asked his relatives and they said he should certainly go to hospital. Should you now overrule the patient's wishes and send him in?

Alternatively, he replied 'Yes' but the relatives said 'No' or both said 'Yes' but none of the men would agree to carry him. Should you force them to by impossible threats of arrest and imprisonment? You would look silly if they called your bluff, but you knew that they wouldn't so long as you could summon up enough fire and brimstone from within you and not falter for a second.

Were they just idle and callous about the patient? Sometimes, perhaps. But there were other possibilities. That they knew more about gangrene than I did and knew that the patient would die in any event and that the village would blame them for not letting him die in his own bed or, less reasonably, for causing his death by the rough journey.

Public opinion in an African village of forty or fifty people can be a terrible scourge, but the antagonism of the ancestral spirits or of a witchdoctor can be far worse. Accidents or illnesses do not happen by chance. They may be inflicted by one of the spirits who has taken offence about something, or by a powerful witchdoctor's spell. The proper procedure may be to propitiate the spirit, or pay the witchdoctor to remove the spell. To interfere with this procedure by carrying the patient off to the white men's hospital could be very dangerous. The carriers might be struck down by the thwarted ancestral ghost or by the witchdoctor.

Were you justified in forcing people to take an action against their superstitious—in effect religious—beliefs? The decision was not easy to make when you were upset at the sight of a man suffering terribly, and also angry at your own inability to help him. My usual decision was to do what the patient wanted and to be quite unpleasant to anyone who wanted to do anything else and refused to help.

Mental sickness presented a different problem. There was no mental hospital or home anywhere in the Protectorate. There was one in Southern Rhodesia and several existed in South Africa but it was very difficult to get a place in any of them. A dangerous lunatic therefore had to be kept in gaol—there was provision in the law for this—unless or until a place for him could be found.

Nobody wanted to send a madman to prison if it could be avoided, so the tendency was to leave a rather greater number of insane persons to the care of relatives than was safe for the community, which reacted with harsh measures to protect itself.

Again decisions had to be made, and in such cases there was no help to be had by asking a mad patient what he wanted. Once, on tour, I came across an alleged homicidal maniac in the bush outside a village. The local blacksmith had welded a leg iron round his ankle with a chain attached to a spike driven through a heavy ironwood log. The man could only move by picking up the log, staggering a few paces with it, stopping for rest and starting again. His relatives took him food once a day.

I expect the poor fellow was incurable, but it was clear that if he was curable his present treatment was unlikely to help. At least he would get reasonable food and shelter and clothing in gaol (which was where the relatives wanted him) while I pestered headquarters to pester the Southern Rhodesian and South African governments to find room for him in a more suitable establishment. I don't know if they ever did as I was soon transferred to another part of the territory.

We managed to get the log and chain off him, but could not cut through the ankle band, and took him back to the Boma, an eight-day march. I ordered the Messengers to take it in turns to stay awake at night to guard him. For the first time in my life, almost the only time, I slept very badly, and so apparently did my unfortunate lunatic. Night after night every time I got up to peep through the tent flaps he seemed to be glaring at me across the camp fire, his eyeballs as red as the fire, with all the Messengers cocooned and asleep in their blankets.

CHAPTER SEVEN

Civilization

Tom had gone on Home leave, leaving me to hand over the District to his successor, who arrived a week or two later in a bad temper in which he remained for the two months of his stay at Serenje. He was sent after this time to Fort Jameson as Provincial Commissioner, the job which he thought he should have had before.

'Handing over' involved counting the cattle, the Boma herd. Counting a herd of long-horned native cattle confined in a kraal is neither an easy nor a soothing occupation. The beasts get nervous and suspicious and mill around with their horns clashing. I had never been a cattle fancier but I knew how many beasts there ought to be, from Tom's list.

My new D.C. walked boldly into the kraal. I followed, closing the kraal entrance behind me. The D.C. tried to count the cattle and I pretended to try to count the cattle. When we left the kraal we had some difficulty in replacing the logs across the gap in the tree trunk wall of the kraal because of the network of freedom-seeking horns.

'Well? What do you make them?' he snapped.

'Dead right, Sir. Same as the list.'

'Nonsense. I made it three short. But you can't count them properly inside the kraal. You should count them on their way out. They can only come out one at a time.'

'Two' I said, from experience. I should have said more than two. I removed the logs from the gap. The D.C. stood on one side of it. I stood on the other. The cattle had been kept in the kraal too late in the morning, waiting for the count. Their stomachs told them that they should have been out grazing by then.

They came out two by two at first. 'Two, four, six, eight . . .' said my new master. But the pressure behind the leaders was too great and white ants had fed cunningly, under the surface of the entrance posts, which, having no heart to resist, broke.

'Eleven, fifteen, twenty-one—no twenty,' cried the D.C., as the cattle swarmed around us, horns clashing *en passant*. Then some of them—'most unusual this' I thought—turned to try to get back into the kraal, as though they had forgotten something that they vitally needed. Then I saw my Airedale, whom I had left asleep in the office. He was always a light sleeper and had an inquisitive nature. Cattle do not like dogs. A period of some confusion followed. At the end of it, with all the cattle stampeding for the bush, I said, 'I'm sure the number is correct, Sir. But I'll get the herdsman, he can check.'

'Can he count?'

'With the clerk, Sir.'

'Very well.'

The new D.C. strode off to count something else. I gave Tom's list to the native clerk. Tom's lists of things were always roughly right. The clerk witnessed the list as correct.

When the new D.C. left, his replacement—an amiable man who refused to count anything but signed everything—stayed rather less than two months and again I was alone, waiting for somebody more permanent and also for my leave.

A lorry arrived. From it stepped the new D.C., in a Saville Row suit and a smart trilby, with the ambience of the West End still surrounding him. He did not want to count anything either. He wanted to talk about his adventures on leave. But I was impatient for my own. I gave the lorry driver a bed for the night and we left at sunrise.

We met the railway line at Kapiri Mposhi just before the bar opened, which event was determined entirely by when its owner awakened from his afternoon sleep. He committed suicide some years later, for no apparent reason. He was a nice man. He probably just got bored with Kapiri. Anybody would.

But to me on that day, Kapiri was civilization. An hotel, with a bar and white men to talk to. Water that came out of taps instead of buckets brought up from a rather muddy stream. Across the road, a railway with a real steam engine shunting some trucks. And tomorrow there would be the mail train, carrying white people who spoke English; iced beer and delectable food.

The signs of civilization were all around me. There were two enormous corrugated iron sheds by the railway line, some tin shed houses and an office for the railway staff, a steel tower with a big water tank on top and a steel windmill with a pump bringing sparkling water up from a borehole; and, dear God, two Indian stores full of chocolate and biscuits and boots and cotton dresses and shirts and tins of soup and enamel chamberpots and everything you could possibly want.

Outside one of them the Indian proprietor was hovering over a barber's chair at the side of the earth road, cutting a white man's hair. At Serenje mine had been cut with a pair of kitchen scissors and the aid of a hand mirror. The results were a bit patchy.

Somebody shouted 'Bar's open' and I moved in. The bar was a separate building, small, but actually built of bricks, presumably in recognition of its important social status. Behind it a whitewashed clay-walled terrace was divided into double rooms. I found a small scorpion in mine, slipping about in the enamel wash basin.

The company in the bar, mostly shunters and platelayers, was splendid, except for one man, a little fellow whose name was Mad Jack, whom everybody kept telling to cheer up. He was, I learned, addicted to the playful use of firearms when in drink, and was occasionally tempted by the railway water tank. It was a target he could hardly miss from the hotel, so long as he was able to stand up and level his rifle. The water spouted splendidly out of the bullet holes and cascaded prettily down around the tower.

But Mad Jack's pleasure at this sight was not shared by the station foreman, who had hitherto grudgingly accepted Jack's apologies and his offer to solder up the holes as soon as the water level sank below them but who had recently decided that enough was enough and had reported Jack to Railway Headquarters down at Broken Hill. Jack was expecting a visit from the police.

'Some people,' the proprietor of the hotel, who was also the barman, told me, 'think it is a bit unsporting of the foreman, but I don't. Anyway Jack needs a lesson before he gets into serious trouble. There was a commercial traveller from Johannesburg up here the other night. I had to put him into Jack's room, in the only bed left. Jack was out, having a few drinks with friends in the railway quarters. He got back to his room about dawn, saw this chap asleep in bed and put a bullet through the roof to wake him up and another into the wall above the bed for luck. The chap bolted through the door in his pyjamas, across the road where the south-bound Kaffir mail was lying in a siding, waiting for the north train to cross. He hopped into it and stayed there for a bit and then woke me to get his suitcase for him. He won't come back here again.'

We adjourned from the bar to a dinner of reedbuck soup, reedbuck stew and pawpaw. Delicious. Back in the bar we played pontoon. I soon found it necessary to ask the man next to me to play my hands for me. He must have had a hard head and great integrity. I found much more money in my trousers pocket in the morning than there was before, including a very shakily written cheque which I had no doubt would have been honoured had it ever been presented, but I tore it up.

The mail train refused to accept my crate of otter skins, leopard skins and varied hunting trophies. 'Foot-and-mouth disease regulations,' said the station foreman, nastily.

'They never reached Serenje' I countered.

'Serenje? Where's that?' he asked. 'Wherever it is, you'll have to leave that crate . . . we'll burn it for you' he added generously. 'You can take that bundle of spears and bows and arrows and things. Get them in the van quick, before the train moves off. She's running late.'

So my mother lost her otter-skin coat and her leopard-skin coat. But she would, I thought, at least have the pleasure of adorning the walls of the front parlour with exotic weapons. In the event, she decided against it. 'They're very nice, dear' she said. 'I'll keep them in the attic for you.'

Nobody on the train knew or cared what had been happening in the outside world during the last two-and-a-half years. Radio receivers had not yet penetrated the Protectorate. Diamond drillers and construction workers from the Congo border region told me about the coming exploitation of vast copper deposits, but showed little interest in my accounts of tribal law and custom.

Neither did anybody on the ship. They were interested in having a good time—and so was I. Africa, I reflected, seemed a very dull continent. Certainly Northern Rhodesia was. Why should anybody be interested in it? Why should I ever return to it? Where was the glamour in an Empire of bucket latrines and biting insects, dirt, disease and poverty? What was I doing in it? Maintaining law and order and impartial justice among primitive tribesmen, many still wearing skins and barkcloth; doing what I could for them in a schoolmasterish, dictatorial way, because there was no other. London's Metropolitan Police would do the job as well as I did, and probably better.

I was wasting the best years of my life. Wine, women and song, and interesting work like writing plays, or making impassioned speeches in wig and gown to an enthralled jury—this was the life for a young man. But I lacked the talents and qualifications for these occupations and there was security in the Colonial Service. I had better stay in it.

All this was a reaction to having spent too long on a remote outstation and to the realization that building up an Empire for the benefit of its peoples and the greater glory of Britain required bricks; and, at least as far as Northern Rhodesia was concerned, there were very few bricks. It was a disillusionment that attacked me periodically for the next two or three years until I came to love the country (I had a house with water-borne sanitation by then) and to have at least a dawning understanding of its people and a sympathy for them which stemmed partly from teaching them how to play football while avoiding treading on their bare feet with my studded boots.

The gaiety of the voyage from Cape Town to the Albert Docks in London was marred by tragedy. The swimming bath on the ship was a canvas affair, lashed along one side from the rail of the boat deck to the rail of the promenade deck. I was up and out on deck a little too early for a swim one morning, watching a sailor rig the bath and waiting for it to be filled.

It was a beautiful morning, with the sun just above the horizon glinting on the blue waves and scattering gold into the white crests and the foam of the bow wave. The ship, dawn clean, seemed to tremble with the excitement of a new day's run, alone, in its unbounded element.

The Bosun appeared just as the sailor had finished. He was a middle-aged man, kindly and very conscientious about his work. He eyed the canvas of the bath and observed that one corner of it was slack. He untied the rope and tried to tighten it while standing in-board on the lower rung of the rail, but the canvas at his back hampered him. So he stood on top of the rail leaning outboard with the whole weight of his body on the rope. It snapped.

I immediately witnessed my first lesson in the incredible

efficiency of seamen. On the instant, the sailor, yelling 'Man overboard', was running down the deck hurling lifebuoys hooked from the rail over the side, with a selectivity that I did not realize at the time—one with a smoke flare, one with a winking red light, but none with an attached rope, which would have been useless. Simultaneously it seemed, the engines stopped, the ship heeled over, swerving to circle. There were bellowed orders from the bridge, rushing feet and the rattle of davits being swung out. A lookout man was running to the forepeak, another climbing up to the crow's nest and crews were assembling at a lifeboat swung out starboard and another swung out port. The ship pursued a wide circle under her own momentum. The boats were lowered as soon as the slackening momentum permitted. Passengers and crew lined the rails searching that beautiful and now damnable sea, glittering and choppy with a movement and a dazzle that defied straining eyes.

The two boats made for the lifebuoys, which would have been invisible by then but for the smoke flare. Others were lowered and searched slowly along the wake of the ship. It had stopped, with a brief throbbing of engines in reverse, exactly where it had started to circle, by the lifebuoys.

The search was long and thorough. Sadly the boats were recalled. As the first was hooked to its davits two of its crew yelled and dived. The bosun's body was just floating up from under the ship's keel, where it had been held by suction while the ship was still moving.

It was obvious that after such a long time artificial respiration would be hopeless but neither this nor the appalling gash in the bosun's head deterred the bosun's shipmates from trying. He was dead, the doctor said later, before he hit the water. His head had struck a scuttle on the way down: there was no water in his lungs.

He was buried at sea next day, after a heartbreaking little service conducted by the Captain. As his encanvassed body slid into that dancing blue water I thought I should never like the sea again. I never have.

Five months leave would have bored me if I had not decided to read law at Lincoln's Inn on this and my next leave, and so be called to the Bar. None of my friends in England were at all interested in hearing about Northern Rhodesia. To them the Empire was a vague sort of halo for Britain, illustrating the greatness of its people, including themselves. Gilded temples and bejewelled elephants topped with velvet canopies indicated its wealth: tea was one of its best products. The Empire was a very good thing . . . and quite interesting, in a way, when you thought of it. But had I seen the Arsenal playing Tottenham Hotspur last Saturday? An amazing game. That new Arsenal goalkeeper was a marvel. Nothing got past him. The Arsenal was a certainty for the Cup.

The only serious interest in Africa, or the Empire generally, that I could discover was quite unreal. It came from the generous hearts and rather bemused minds of members of the Fabian Society and of the Aborigines Protection Society, who seemed to think that the native populations were ground down under the spurred heels of British administrators' riding boots.

I was taken to see dog racing under the arc lamps of the New Cross track, and to the dirt track motor cycle races, which also bored me and the incessant roar of the engines gave me a headache. Epsom, however, was better. There at least was fresh air and sunshine, and superior looking horses whose energies were skilfully directed by clever little men in bright colours and whose bottoms, I noticed with surprise, never seemed to touch the saddles.

It was at Epsom that I made a new friend whose way of life I greatly envied and should have followed. He possessed a large and powerful car in which we drove, after he had collected his Epsom winnings, to his house on the Hampshire coast. He made a fat living from backing horses and fishing for lobsters, and had evolved a formula for success in both professions.

As to racing, it was essential, he explained, always to back on the course just before the race started when the odds had settled down. You must then back the second favourite. It would not, of course, always win, but more often than not, it would. 'And you don't pay income tax on your winnings,' he added cheerfully.

He took me out in his rowing boat in the late afternoon, launching it from the holidaymakers' sweeping sandy beach.

'We'll row out to the rocks,' he said, 'where my pots are.'

'What rocks?' I asked. 'I can't see any.'

'You never will, not even at low tide. But I know where they are. I was born here.'

That did not seem to me to qualify him for bathyscopic insight into the sea bed, but he rowed his way miraculously through the waste of waves to the corks of his widely scattered lobster pots. We pulled them up, filled a sack with more than a dozen large lobsters and rowed back.

We then made the round of the bars of the town's most expensive hotels, taking the dripping sack with us.

'How many do you want?' he would ask the barman.

'Three today, the boss said.'

Three very live and angry lobsters would then be passed over the counter, handled with equal skill both by my friend and the barman, and paid for out of the barman's till. A health would then be drunk and so to the next bar until the sack was empty.

It seemed to me to be a laborious and rather inebriated way of selling lobsters until my friend observed, 'This way you don't pay income tax'.

I had never paid any income tax as my salary level in Northern Rhodesia was below the generous line drawn by those of my Colonial Service colleagues who advised the Government on fiscal affairs. For the first time I realized that income tax in England was of some importance. I agreed with my friend that it was also iniquitous, particularly in regard to the proceeds of lobsters, hard won from the sea.

I sailed back to Africa wondering whether it would not have been better for me to have resigned from the Colonial Service and taken a temporary job in London until I had saved enough money to buy a rowing boat.

CHAPTER EIGHT

The Capital City

I HAD EXPECTED to return to Serenje and was surprised to be posted to Lusaka. Transfers of administrators from one district to another were too frequent. We were few in number, and sickness and overseas leave made transfers inevitable, but they were a serious handicap to our trusteeship administration, in Africa as elsewhere. A District Officer was often just beginning to get close to his local tribesmen, to learn their language really well, to know their tribal laws and customs and to understand their geographical and agricultural problems after a year or two in the area, when he was transferred to another district hundreds of miles away with a different tribe, a different language and different problems.

However, after the isolation of Serenje I was content with my new posting to a town Boma. Lusaka was now in the process of becoming the new capital of Northern Rhodesia, being cooler, more healthy and more central than Livingstone. Apart from a scatter of government houses and offices on what was known as Snob's Hill, the town consisted of an earth road with a waggon track alongside it, running parallel to the railway line, beyond which were the railwaymen's quarters and the native compounds. In the dry season the road looked as though it had been shelled by light artillery; in the rains it was a quagmire. It was called Cairo Road, and, like the railway, it would have reached Cairo if Rhodes's dream had been practicable.

Lusaka was typical of the dozen or so little European settlements spaced out along the railway line up to the Congo border. Its existence was justified only by the farms and ranches spread out over some thirty miles around it and by the need for an administrative centre for the province which included several large native reserves. It was now expanding out into the bush on the hill as the new capital began to take shape. Its population was growing rapidly.

The Flag-Wagger

At erratic intervals along Cairo Road, the corrugated iron roofs of the Boma, the Grand Hotel, two or three general stores, a butchery, a bank, Counsell's Hotel and a few offices and oddments grumbled metallically as they contracted or expanded according to the temperature. Nearby, lost in the long grass, was a hospital.

The Grand Hotel, like all the hotels of the time, was built around a large bar. The bar was built first, some rooms for the accommodation of those who could not find their way home followed, and finally a dining room was added, to provide the stabilizing influence of food.

Outside the Grand was a hitching rail for horses and the unlimited open bushland for outspanning the farmers' waggon teams. Counsell's Hotel was generally considered to be rather more respectable than the Grand and its long bar was favoured by civil servants and other members of the upper crust who sometimes wore long trousers instead of shorts, and, occasionally, even ties.

It was in this bar that Willie, the headmaster of the little European School, and I, drank a pig.

I cycled in, ahead of my carriers, along a dusty track after a long tour of the Soli Reserve, arriving at Counsell's a little before noon on a blazing hot Saturday, parched and exhausted.

Except for the barman, 'Speck', and Willie, who did not work on Saturdays, the bar was empty. Willie took one look at me and said 'Give him a beer, Speck, quick'. In due course I returned the compliment and my thoughts, no longer concentrating entirely on thirst, turned to the problem of the pig. It had been given to me by a Soli Chief, to whom, after a decent interval, I had presented its market price in cash. It was being escorted into Lusaka, on the end of a string, by the leading carrier in my retinue.

I did not want this pig any more than it wanted me, and I was wondering what on earth to do with it when it appeared, as in about an hour it would, trotting down the main street followed by twenty-two singing carriers. Speck, I now remembered, had once been a butcher; the hotel could probably do with a pig.

'How many beers will you give me for a pig, Speck?' I asked.

He looked surprised and replied severely 'You haven't got no pig'.

'I have' I said. 'How many beers for it?'

Speck, now very suspicious, asked 'Where is it and how big is it?'

'It will be along soon,' I told him, 'and it's about so long, so high, and so broad.'

Speck considered the dimensions indicated, and said 'Ten'.

I asked him to set them up on the bar, and Willie and I started on them, while I explained how the pig was honestly come by. There were still several beers left on the counter when we heard the carriers approaching.

'You'll have to give me a hand with it, Willie,' I said. We carried the violently protesting pig through the swing doors and dumped it on the counter for Speck, but he was too slow. The pig joined him behind the bar. It was an exceedingly agile pig and by the time it was recaptured the shelves of liquor at the back of the bar had suffered severe loss. Speck and the pig, both disgruntled and voluble, disappeared into the back yard.

With the pig disposed of, the day wore on until nearly teatime, when Willie suddenly remembered he was supplying the band for a dance at Broken Hill that night. Ninety miles would take him about five hours, such was the state of the road, and he must hurry off. The band consisted of a small pile of precious gramophone records placed neatly on the seat next to the driver's. Willie got into the wrong side of the car and sat on them.

We sorted things out and found several records which were not cracked right across.

'They'll do' said Willie. 'It won't matter.'

It didn't. Just outside town there was a nasty twist in the track and a culvert of logs over a stream. Willie missed the culvert and the car could not be repaired until Monday.

Unusual things always seemed to happen when Willie was around. He was the sort of chap who attracted disaster. I went to call on my friend Paddy Byrne, of the Public Works Department, on another fateful Saturday. Paddy was sharing a bungalow with a Stock Inspector called Gerald, whom I also knew well. I did not know that Willie had recently been added to the menage. The bungalow had a broad mosquito-gauzed verandah running right round its four main rooms, the back part of the verandah serving as pantry and store.

Paddy, staring straight ahead, passed me as I opened the front door. Fat and perspiring, he was trotting along the verandah clad in a bath towel and holding a large carving knife at the ready. As he passed me, he muttered, 'I'll kill the bastard'.

Before he reappeared on his circuit, I heard complaining noises from a bedroom. Gerald, I found, was sitting on his bed, loudly despairing the futility of the world and announcing his intention to end it all. His rifle was between his knees.

I removed it and said, 'Wait until you've had a last drink, at least. I'll get you one.' I dropped the gun in the next room and trotted quietly and at a discreet distance after Paddy on his rounds.

As I passed the meat safe (a large wooden frame on legs with a mosquito-gauzed door), I thought I heard a hoarse whisper. On the next circuit, I was certain I heard it, but trotted on, baffled as to its source. Nobody could be in the meat safe, I reasoned, it was too small. On the third round the whisper was louder, more urgent. I stopped, looked quickly through the gauze, and said 'Stay there'.

I then reversed direction and stopped Paddy, who was tiring. 'Who are you after, Paddy?' I asked.

He looked at me vaguely and then with recognition.

'Willie' he said grimly.

'Little man, dark hair?' I enquired.

'That's him. Bloody little Scotsman. Called me a bog-trotter. I'll kill him unless he apologizes. Where is he? I can't find him anywhere but I know the bastard's here.'

'He's well away by now' I said. 'I passed him as I arrived. He was running down the drive.'

'Was he?' Paddy started to laugh. 'I've scared hell out of him then. Have a drink.'

'And one for Gerald' I said. 'Get him out on the stoep. He needs company.'

The three of us were soon in good spirits.

'Willie' I said, 'is in the meat safe.'

'What the devil is he doing in there?' asked Paddy in amazement. 'Willie,' he roared, 'come and have a drink.'

Willie, creased and humble, approached cautiously.

'Sorry, Paddy' he mumbled.

'What for?' said Paddy, perplexed. 'Has everybody gone round the bend? What have you been doing in the meat safe?'

Paddy still lives. Willie, the dapper but sometimes aggressive little man, with too sharp edged a wit, died young.

Gerald was eaten by a lion. He and Paddy, on their way to Fort

Jameson, stayed the night at the Rufunsa Rest Camp—a few wattle-and-daub thatched huts, backed by forested hills, looking across a wide plain to a hazy horizon. The Rest Camp capitao warned them that there was a man-eater about. But Paddy and Gerald, reckless and fearless as always, decided that it was too hot a night to keep the hut door shut. They slept side by side under their mosquito nets. The lion ripped Gerald's net away and carried him off. Gerald made no sound. Paddy was awakened only by the ripping of the net and the crashing of the stretcher bed, but he recognized the stink of the beast, which must have got Gerald by the neck and broken it. 'I like to think Gerald knew nothing about it,' Paddy told me. By the time he had fumbled his way out of his mosquito net and scrabbled for matches, lamp and gun, it was too late to do anything effective on a pitch dark night. He set off on the spoor at first light. About all he found was Gerald's middle finger with the signet ring on it, and his head.

He and Paddy were a rather wild pair, but both spent long periods in the bush, Paddy supervising the construction of wooden bridges and earth roads, and Gerald, who was particularly good at his job, patiently breaking down the peasants' resistance to dipping tanks, inoculation, culling and animal husbandry, which, so slowly, helped some of them to improve their herds and their incomes.

My sympathy for both the black and the white farmers grew with an increasing knowledge of what they were up against: sub-tropical pests and diseases, a seven-month annual drought and a wet season when the rain fell in sometimes destructive torrents. But I did not realize how hard nature could hit at years of continued effort until the locusts came.

They were heralded by some startling posters hurriedly printed by the Government Printer and stuck up all over the place by the Department of Agriculture. Headed 'National Emergency', they warned of a huge locust invasion sweeping down through South-Central Africa, and gave some advice on how to combat it by banging drums and dustbin lids and petrol tins, and shouting. The aim was to drive them off the crops and into the bush. Some supplies of a locust-killing insecticide were being railed up from South Africa. My Provincial Commissioner had his own ideas on the menace and he summoned me to his house late one evening.

'I have information,' he said, 'that the breeding ground of the locusts is in the Kafue swamps. Go and find the place and destroy the damn things. And bring back some specimens in a tin. There's some doubt as to whether they are red locusts or brown. Start off tonight, as soon as you can.'

This seemed to me an impossible task. I had a vision of setting out on a bicycle with a fly switch, a compass and a haversack of iron rations and ending up in a grave of liquid mud. But the P.C. had made the necessary preparations for me.

'There will be a lorry at your house, with carriers, messengers, camp equipment and some boxes of dusting powder for the locusts. The powder is poisonous. You must not inhale it. When you and the carriers use it you must make pads of something to cover your mouths and nostrils.'

At this time no swarm had appeared in Lusaka or in the district. I supposed that I could dust locusts with as much success as anybody else, and set off with great enthusiasm engendered by the national crisis. It seemed odd to me that the breeding ground should be some seventy miles west of Lusaka, when the invasion was said to be approaching from Tanganyika in the North, but the P.C., I thought, must know what he was talking about.

The lorry rattled and bounced through the farms. We slept from 2 a.m. till dawn, pushed on again and reached the outermost farm about noon, where a young bachelor farmer offered to accompany us. We reached the edge of the Kafue swamps at dusk and camped on rising ground overlooking them.

At dawn I looked at the scenery and then at the sketch map the P.C. had given me. The scenery was impressive; the map, empty except for the names of a few villages, was not. There was no neat cross to mark the breeding spot of locusts.

The sun, about to rise behind us, was colouring the empty sky with those indefinable shades of green and blue and mauve and pink above the gilt edge of the eastern horizon. Ahead the limitless green plain of tall grass seemed to come to life as the sun edged up, tipping the grass with pale gold as it waved in the dawn breeze.

It all looked very beautiful from a distance. But ploughing through it, in up to a foot of water and mud, with the grass over our heads, soaked to the skin with dew, showered with small biting insects, and being cut on arms and legs by sharp-edged grass blades, produced a different impression.

Clearly no locust breeding ground existed. Interested villagers listened politely, giving no sign of amusement at the harmless madness of the Bwanas, and directed us on to the next hamlet.

Incredibly, we at last found a headman who knew where the locusts were but was baffled as to why we wanted to look at them. We camped at his village, on dry land, and he led us next morning to the place of locusts which, I was delighted to find after a few miles of bog-trotting, was also on dry land. It was a raised area in the swamp, a little spongy and covered with short grass. There were a good many locusts scattered about, nibbling grass, but hardly a thick swarm.

The inevitable difficulties arose over explaining, with the assistance of a Messenger, the purpose of our expedition. Here we were, I endeavoured to proclaim, at the heart of the greatest menace that had ever threatened the country. These flying things had come from a far-off land, to breed in untold millions and eat the country bare. When had they arrived?

'They've always been here.'

'But don't you do anything about them?'

'Sometimes we collect them and eat them. They're very good fried—much fat.'

'Are there more this year than ever before?'

'No, about the same.'

This seemed very disheartening, and I could see no signs of the locusts breeding. Eating seemed to be their only interest. I asked the headman when was their breeding time.

'Now,' he said, and wandered about digging his finger in the soil here and there with an unerring eye, exposing little wriggling hoppers. He obviously knew more about his locusts than the P.C. did.

I collected two or three and put them in a cigarette tin and we dusted locusts until the powder ran out, without much effect on their numbers. It occurred to me to tell the headman not to eat any for some time, because of the poison. He nodded and said, 'We never eat any that have died. You never know what they have died of.'

The results of the expedition, for me, were a dose of malaria, a few veldt sores from grass cuts and swamp infection, and a commendation from the P.C.

'They are red locusts' I told him, opening the tin and displaying their colour.

'Just what the Agricultural Department said they would be' he said, beaming. He kept them, and from the satisfied look on his face at the time I wouldn't be surprised if they were still amongst his souvenirs. I thought he would be depressed at my evidence that their abode could hardly be the breeding place of the approaching invasion, but he was not.

'We've discovered that they come from Tanganyika, Lake Rukwa, or somewhere,' he said, confidentially.

Come they certainly did, and when they came I realized the full futility of dusting their tails. They flew over high, like a wide swathe of brown smoke, from the horizon. They circled, sinking and sinking, and settled, towards sunset. At a little distance, the trees seemed to be a mass of pink blossom. Close up to the branches you could watch the locusts' jaws moving and actually hear the sound of community munching.

In the early morning the pale light glistened on their wings, and until they rose the trees seemed to be covered with hoar frost—a beautiful sight. They took flight and the trees were naked, without a leaf.

The trees around Lusaka did not matter. The crops of the white farmers and the African subsistence peasants did. I spent the next few months either uselessly fighting locusts or more usefully estimating the extent of famine relief measures that would be needed in the villages.

The Africans, with their very small holdings were, up to a point, better able to cope with the plague than the Europeans with their wide lands of maize or wheat. 'Every man for himself' was the watchword. If you could make enough noise to drive the locusts off your land, it was up to your neighbour to do the same when they settled on his, until theoretically they were driven into the bush to less succulent but uninterrupted feeding. However, the locusts believed in nothing but the best.

With tireless effort and incessant din, something might have been saved from the flying swarms. *Nothing* could be saved from the hoppers. If a crop was in the line of their advance, that was the end of it. The hoppers, about two inches long, could not fly off until they matured, even if they wanted to.

One description of a pitched battle with hoppers will be enough; they were all alike. The Northern Rhodesia Regiment, equipped with entrenching tools, were spread out across two farms attempting to stem the hordes of invading hoppers by digging trenches in front of them. Not, as I first thought, in the hope that the hoppers would break their little necks by falling into the trenches, but that they would either be baulked by them and change course towards the bush, or could be more easily powdered by the trench-full. The hoppers did not change direction, but extended their left flank on to a third farm, which the Regiment could not defend. Reserves were called up—me.

I pitched my tent in the rear of the invaders (the canvas and the scuffled clearing was soon thick with stragglers and crawling wounded) and squelched with my labourers across the invading hordes to link up with the army, which had just conducted a small tactical retreat to dig new trenches, their previous ones having been over-run. We dug until the enemy were tentatively chewing at our boots and then stood back to watch. It was, I had just learned, a waste of time to use the poison powder out of the large Vim-shaped tins, until the trench was full. The locusts underneath were squashed or suffocated by the ones on top, but the powder on the top layer was picked up by the first two or three dozen ranks that crossed the full trench—not that it made much difference, with millions and millions of ranks behind.

The advance was silent, faintly odorous (hoppers have a vague, over-ripe vegetable smell) and totally fantastic. The living carpet of green, brown-striped, moved forward at about the speed of a large caterpillar, as if from an enormous production line in an invisible factory. Nothing could stop it, or turn it, except annihilation. It had no will or reason, only the mammoth power of the instinct of its destiny: to eat, to fly, to breed and to die. By the grace of God, I thought, locusts are not interested in eating people.

The advance, so slow, seemed swift as it reached our trenches, hurriedly dug to a depth of about two feet. A slow-motion cataract of hoppers filled the trench, and the carpet moved across it. I stayed to watch them while another defence line was dug. There was something totally irrelevant about them, neither good nor bad, neither concerned nor unconcerned with life or death, just dream things from another world. I am glad I saw them but I have no desire to see them again.

The locusts moved on towards their destiny with quiet persistence. Where they had passed, and fortunately this was not all over the country, they left bare farms and bankrupt farmers behind them.

To the peasant farmers it was food, and not money, that was important—food and their home-brewed beer, made from malted grain. As always, the villager's hope of getting something for nothing complicated the task of the relief workers. Villages which the locusts had never visited claimed to be eaten out; others which had salvaged a fair crop, claimed to be starving. Others soon would in fact be starving. When in doubt, the acid test was to lift the roofs off the grain-bins circling the village. Some were full, others fairly full (one preached a lesson on 'less beer this year'), and others were empty. The latter had to be filled—or rather maize had to be supplied in sacks, from the famine relief vote.

Fortunately, perhaps, in the long run, this explosion of red locusts affected a good many countries besides Northern Rhodesia and attracted serious international attention. Years of research and hard work in the field, by the International Red Locust Control organisation, have, it is said, so nearly eliminated them in their Rukwa breeding grounds, which are still closely watched, that they can never be a menace again. But I wouldn't trust them.

The Provincial Commissioner, thinking perhaps that if I could locate a small settlement of breeding locusts in the vast Kafue plains then I must have the unusual ability of seeing through miles of elephant grass, decided that I could assist in the layout of the new capital by finding a suitable site for an African Trades School.

'Somewhere about there' he said, putting a finger on a large blank space on a sketch map which contained little more than the outlines of the sites of Government House and the Secretariat.

The area was about two miles from the Boma, so I took a gun as well as a compass and shot a duiker in the bush before reaching the belt of seven foot high grass, which seemed to be about where the finger had indicated. With the Messenger and a few labourers I wandered around the place, pushing the grass aside.

At least the area seemed to be flat, so we stuck a tall bush pole in the ground, followed the compass in a fairly straight line for the required distance, stuck in another pole, turned at a right angle and continued the proceedings until four poles marked the site where the Trades School, later a Technical College, now stands. In the next few days the labourers cut the grass on the site. The Provincial Commissioner inspected and approved it.

It was about the last of my activities that he did approve. Two incidents soured him, though both were his own fault. The first concerned the building of a dam across the Chongwe River in the Sala tribal area outside Lusaka. My part in this venture was confined to explaining to the villagers what a boon the dam would be for them and their cattle, so as to encourage them to provide the labour to work on it. I then had to see that the labour was paid and fed in accordance with the contract. The design and construction of the dam was, thank God, the contractor's affair.

The villagers were not at first impressed with the idea. They and their cattle had survived without a dam. I finally sold them the idea with fish. The dam would be stocked with fish which they would be able to scoop out with nets or fish traps.

The dam, when completed, was a splendid sight. It seemed to me to be unnecessarily big for so small a river—the Chongwe was only some twenty or thirty yards wide, bone-dry and full of smallish boulders during the time the dam was built. The boulders should have warned the contractor of the fall of the river and the torrent which it must produce to bring them downstream. The rains opened with the usual violent storm and the usual comment that it was the worst in living memory. The dam was washed straight down the river. Fortunately I was never required to visit the Sala area again and so never had to go back to the area and explain the absence of fish to the villagers. The Provincial Commissioner never actually accused me of sabotage but he made it plain that I was not the man he had thought me to be.

The second incident concerned a local farmer and was responsible for the final breach between us. The farmer had complained about the position of a native village. He said it was on his land, and had convinced the Provincial Commissioner of this. I was sent to make a survey of the position of the village. I did the job and gave the P.C. a tracing. The village was nearly half a mile off the farm. I told the P.C. how pleased I was about that since all the land in the region had once been African-occupied and that the villagers had been turned off it by the British South Africa Company administration to make way for European farms. The P.C. was not pleased. He called me back after telephoning the farmer, and asked me slyly if I had taken bearings from the farm and from the village, as instructed.

'No' I said. 'It's hilly country. You can't see the village from the farm, or the farm from the village, so I sweated up to the beacons on the tops of surrounding hills and took a number of cross bearings on both.'

He wrote me a rude minute about incompetence and put a copy of it on my Personal File in his Staff (Confidential) records and sent in a copy to the Secretary for Native Affairs. He then sent out my D.C. to do the job. On his return, the D.C. brought his tracing to me first and asked if I had a copy of mine—he was taking no chances. I said I would swop him my copy for a copy of his. We then put one on top of the other and his black dot marking the village fitted mine beautifully.

He put his tracing in to the P.C. and I waited. Nothing happened. So I pinned both tracings together, added the P.C.'s rude minute and sent the lot to him with a rude note of my own. He didn't like that. Tact was never my strong point.

Nor, at this stage, was Law, but as I had now been upgraded to a Magistrate of the Third instead of Fourth Class, it was inevitable that I should appear on the bench sooner or later. I did not look forward to this. There were experienced police prosecutors and several practising advocates in Lusaka. They would know a great deal more law than I did and I was afraid I would make a fool of myself. But I was greatly heartened by my first case—a civil claim for debt.

An African had bought a sewing machine from a local store on credit and had made no attempt to pay the bill for it. The storekeeper had briefed one of the advocates. I appeared on the dais, bowed gravely, was bowed at in return and sat down with my heart thumping, knowing that a very tricky point of law would come up. It must: because the Credit Sales to Natives Ordinance, promulgated many years before to prevent the simple people from getting into the grip of traders through buying on credit, prohibited the trader from bringing an action for debt of this nature. Obviously the advocate must have spotted a loophole somewhere, or perhaps he was an expert on constitutional law and had found that the Ordinance was *ultra vires*. I decided to take this bull by the horns at once to avoid hours of embarrassment as the advocate unfolded his knotty point of law in the course of the hearing. A casual, almost careless request at the start for an outline of the legal point involved was the line to take. I could then immediately adjourn for ten minutes on some pretext, and consult the District Commissioner or make a desperate attempt to phone the High Court in Livingstone.

'With the provisions of the Credit Sales to Natives in mind,' I said in the confidential tone of one lawyer to another, 'which would normally preclude this claim, it might save time if we dealt first with such points of law as you wish to raise in avoidance of the Ordinance.'

The advocate's eyes opened wide, he blushed, and said, 'My God! I'd forgotten about that, Your Worship. I beg leave to withdraw the claim.'

The D.C., who had pushed the case on to me because he was as scared of lawyers as I was, heard soon afterwards from the advocate that he had been shot down, with biting sarcasm, in the first ten seconds of the case by 'that bumptious youngster'. The D.C. was much impressed and thereafter pushed on to me all cases that fell within my limited powers. Fortunately they were nearly all beneath the dignity of, or unprofitable to, the local advocates.

An early fall was inevitable. It was caused by a house-breaker, a most evasive and voluble liar who pretended when stumped not to understand anything at all. Magistrates should be seen but rarely heard, and should never lose their tempers, but nobody had yet warned me of these maxims, and halfway through the case I broke both of them, roundly accusing the prisoner of trying to cause confusion rather than suffering from it.

When I had finished, the police Inspector prosecuting said, 'I think, Your Worship, the prisoner may be confused. You have not yet read the charge to him and taken a plea.'

So we had to start all over again.

Judging criminals was no pleasure but, thanks to the Head Gaoler, an ex-boxer, I sometimes found myself in a more congenial judicial role.

The Flag-Wagger

The gaoler was to be referee at a boxing tournament to be held in the dining room of the Hotel. Abe, the proprietor of the Grand Hotel, was promoting the fights, and the gaoler asked me to be one of the judges.

'But I know nothing about boxing' I protested. 'I've never been in a ring except as a boy scout and the only instruction I was ever given then was to hit the other boy harder than he hit me.'

'Very sound instruction' said the gaoler. 'That's all there is to it, really. You have a bit of paper with a line down the middle, one side for boxer A and the other for boxer B. Every time one lands a wallop you put down a mark on his side of the paper. At the end, unless one man gets laid out, you tot up the marks and hand them in.'

I at first declined the invitation, feeling that no boxer should be expected to have his prowess judged by me.

'It's all right, there will be three other judges,' said the gaoler. 'We take the average of the marks.'

I said that if he could get three other judges without difficulty he could surely find a fourth, better qualified than I.

The gaoler shook his head. 'I've told Abe I won't referee unless you are one of the judges. You're honest—you have to be, you're a magistrate. Now Abe has put a lot of money on the big fight. He has selected all the other judges. Two of them I know are in his pocket, and I'm a bit doubtful about the third. Abe's man is bound to win, if he's not knocked out, unless at least one of the judges is scoring fairly.' I took his point, and accepted the invitation.

The tournament was rather late in starting, owing to the proprietor's reluctance to close the bar. Nobody could be expected to take his seat around the arena until it was closed. Abe liked his profits both ways.

The (allegedly) big fight was between two professional middleweights, up from South Africa. Nobody had ever heard of them but I think they must have been friends. They certainly went out of their way to avoid hurting each other. The one in blue shorts landed more blows than the other, who was perhaps awarded points by my colleagues for clever defence. At any rate, blue shorts lost on points, though he seemed a clear winner to me.

The amateurs performed more zealously, none better than the local butcher, hadicapped by a large paunch. There was nothing wanting in his physical strength, and had any of his right swings connected he would certainly have won on a knockout. He could not have scored any points for clever defence, for he had none. He went in with both fists, was floored several times, and began to slow up in the third round as his wind troubled him. He took a terrible beating and swore violently when his second threw in the towel.

I was called upon to make a little speech at the end of the evening, and praised the butcher's courage, saying that I had never seen a man with such guts. The roar of laughter from the crowd seemed to me both impolite and unfair to the butcher.

But despite the stimulating social and sporting life and the interesting and varied work which Lusaka had to offer, I decided that I would much rather be back on an outstation far away from a white population of which a considerable percentage were, I realized uneasily, no credit to their race in their treatment of Africans.

Except for the farmers, hardly any of the 'white settlers' were settlers at all. They had come to the Protectorate as traders, miners, railwaymen, and construction workers for much better pay and conditions or profits than they could get at home. There were, at this time, less than fifteen thousand of them. Some stayed for a few years, some stayed for many years, and the latter nearly all returned to their home countries when they had made enough money to retire on.

In general they were not at all interested in the two-and-a-half million Africans, except as cheap labour, nor in the country itself, except for the material gains it had to offer them. They disliked 'Colonial Office' rule, not as a nation of people wishing to govern themselves in their own country, but because it prevented them from exploiting the Protectorate and its indigenous people to the extent which they would have liked.

The South Africans and the Southern Rhodesians brought with them to Northern Rhodesia their *herrenvolk* attitude towards the Africans, and this the immigrants from Britain quickly absorbed. They thought they owned the country and its people and they felt that we of the Colonial Service, fellow white men, should stand together with them instead of protecting the Africans from them. There was not much clamour yet about white settler rule in Northern Rhodesia, but it was soon to grow when a railway worker called Roy Welensky took up the cry, and to lead eventually to the disastrous Federation with Southern Rhodesia, the results of which are still troubling the world today.

Nor at this time, the early 1930s, was there any thought in African minds of self-government, though the Secretary for Native Affairs had already noted in a minute to the Governor that there were signs amongst some of the chiefs and their few educated or semi-educated followers that they would not for long be content to have virtually no say at all in the Government of the Protectorate.

Already the African workers in the towns were beginning to see through the new Europeans who bossed them and abused them in their labour. These Europeans were not like the British South Africa Company administrators and their Colonial Service successors and the missionaries that they had known since the first white penetration in 1900. They had thought that the white men were gods (as President Kaunda said during the struggle for Independence in the 1950s).

In the rural areas they still thought that.

CHAPTER NINE

Back to the Wilds

WHETHER MY WISH for rusticity became known to the Provincial Commissioner and was recommended to the Secretary for Native Affairs with pleasure or whether the latter, in pondering over his little flags on the staff chart decided to move mine to Mpika in the Northern Province, I do not know. But that is where I went for six months, before the pin was moved again to Kasama for a few months and again to Fort Rosebery for two years, with an extended home leave in between which enabled me to sit for the Bar final examinations.

Mpika was 'just another outstation', except for its nearby hotel and airstrip which was a staging post for the first B.O.A.C. African Service of biplanes which had a speed of about 80 knots, and for the unusual honour of a visitation by the Governor, who asked me if the tax collection was going well. Although that was the only official question that Sir Ronald Storrs put to me, his visit was instructive. From it I learned that cocks cannot crow unless their necks are fully extended.

This was explained in a letter from Sir Ronald's Private Secretary, which forewarned us that His Excellency was a very bad sleeper who could never get to sleep until the small hours of the morning and did not take kindly to being awakened half-an-hour later by the unseemly crowing of cocks. H.E. therefore requested that all cocks on the station be confined at night, during his visit, in boxes of insufficient height for them to extend their necks, without which ability they could not crow.

Neither the D.C. nor I kept chickens, but there were plenty in the Messengers' Lines.

'How on earth are we going to explain it all to the Messengers?' I asked the D.C. 'They'll think the man is mad.'

'They think we're all mad anyway' the D.C. answered. 'As long as they box their cocks what does it matter?'

I remember wondering how much interest in or knowledge of our African wards Sir Ronald had. I had met him twice before in Lusaka and his heart seemed to me to be in the Middle East, where he had spent all his previous working life. He was a brilliant classical and oriental scholar, perhaps too brilliant for his down-to-earth task in Northern Rhodesia. He retired after two years in the Protectorate and was succeeded by Sir Hubert Young, who had only four years experience of colonial administration, to which he came from the Army and the Foreign Office via India and the Middle East. The frequent transfer of Governors and the appointment of some of them from other services or from politics was, I believe, a mistaken policy. The best Governors we ever had in Northern Rhodesia were regular Colonial Servicemen with long African experience.

Kasama, though not much more than an outstation, was Provincial Headquarters, with a European staff of six and a few white traders in the little township.

I made a friend of the P.C.'s clerk, a young Londoner on his first tour of service. He arrived at the office one morning rather excited and disturbed, having nearly been shot by a prison warder. He had paid a dawn visit to the P.K. up the little path at the back of his house just before the prisoners came round the station to clear the latrine buckets. One of the prisoners had decided to make a break. The warder had fired wildly. The only thing to be mortally wounded was the bucket, but the clerk had fled, holding up his trousers, much to the delight of the prisoners.

He thought Kasama was a rather adventurous place. So did I. In the course of the next few months the District Commissioner found a leopard occupying his sitting room; I myself had a narrow escape in the blackness of the night, trying to save my dog from a leopard which had sprung over my garden wall; and the Provincial Commissioner had nearly sat on a deadly puff adder coiled up comfortably on the driving seat of his car.

The reason for my transfer to Kasama was that the Provincial Commissioner wished to keep an eye on me. I had met him during a brief stay at his previous station and had committed three sins: I had appeared at dinner in a suit instead of a dinner jacket—(Tom and I had always worn shorts for dinner at Serenje); I had declined his invitation to play tennis because I had a bad cold; and I had had what I thought was an amicable and interesting argument with him about the myths of the Christian religion, which, as a conservative Anglican, he had not enjoyed as much as I had.

He had therefore told the Chief Secretary unofficially, on the old boy network, that I was intellectually arrogant (probably correct) and a valetudinarian (incorrect). He thought I should go back to Education.

He was a very decent man and therefore told me all this. He was also a splendid native administrator with a real affection for his charges. He was entranced, one day, when he walked past my house and the baked earth clearing next to it and found me leading the Station Labourers team against the Messengers in a hilarious, but shockingly inept, game of football. He stayed to watch and at the end of the game, grinning broadly, he said, 'I noticed that you were the referee as well as centre forward. Was that quite fair?'

'Somebody had to be referee' I said cheerfully, 'and I am still teaching them the game.'

He said he had noticed that. Then his expression changed; he looked rather embarrassed. He said, abruptly, 'I made a great mistake about you, Franklin, and I shall tell the Chief Secretary so.' He continued on his walk.

Once again, the District Commissioner passed most of the court work on to me, though there was not much of it. There never was on outstations (criminals prefer urban to rural life) but what cases there were did not lack interest.

My first burglar was ushered into the office by a Messenger Interpreter. There were, of course, no lawyers, no police and no court house in Kasama. He squatted on the floor and clapped slowly. Both the sitting down and the slow clapping were normal native custom when meeting a superior—be he a chief or a grandfather or a bwana of the Boma.

He looked quite amiable until after he had pleaded Guilty. I told the Interpreter to explain to him that this was unwise, that since he was not defended it was up to me to see that he got a square deal and that the prosecution witnesses must be made to prove the case against him. He saw no sense in that.

He said crossly 'I did it. Everyone knows I did it. I don't want to waste time listening to all those witnesses.'

'I shall enter a plea of Not Guilty,' I said firmly.

'You can't do that if I say I'm guilty' he argued. 'I'm a burglar. I've always been a burglar. That's my work. You know all about me. Why do you waste my time?'

I did know all about him. I knew he had a long list of previous convictions and I knew that if he were convicted I would have to give him a pretty long stretch . . . and I was beginning to like him.

We argued until I weakened and entered his plea of Guilty, but insisted on hearing the witnesses, or at any rate the first two. He made such a fuss after that, about wasting time, that I gave up.

'All right,' I said, 'I find you guilty and sentence you to two years hard labour.'

He grinned cheerfully and said 'That's better. Now I'll tell you what I'm going to do. I know this Kasama prison. It's the easiest to break out of that I've ever been in, but I'll stay there for three months and then escape at night. Then, first I'll break into the Golf Club, because I want that cloth over all those long cushions. I like that cloth. Then I'll burgle the Education Officer's house. I don't like that man. And the Provincial Commissioner's house. I don't like him either. But I won't burgle yours, don't you worry. You'll be all right. I like you.'

Three months later he did exactly what he said he would, and disappeared from the District. To my regret, I was never able to congratulate him.

Defending a murderer before the Provincial Commissioner—to whom the High Court had delegated its powers for the occasion—was an unexpected experience. On leave I had taken only one preliminary subject at Lincoln's Inn, which was Roman law: not very helpful. The junior District Officer who was prosecuting was a barrister though he had never been in practice. The Provincial Commissioner had arranged his office into some semblance of a court.

The accused had lain in wait, at dawn, for his wife and mother-in-law who were staying at a neighbouring village where, he believed, his wife had committed adultery. As the two women came up the path, he attacked his wife with a heavy stick. The mother-in-law tried to pull him away, but he threw her off, pulled a fishcutting knife from his headload on the side of the road and stabbed his wife to death.

I could see no hope for him until the mother-in-law described how she had grabbed his waist cloth to tug him away, but he had pushed her off and the waist cloth came away in her hand.

'What else was he wearing?' I asked.

'Nothing' she answered.

I knew very little about the tribe and its customs but I heard the hiss of intaken breath and saw the shock on the faces of the Africans in the court as this piece of evidence came out. I asked the Messenger about it when we adjourned for lunch. He told me that for a man to be seen naked by his mother-in-law was a very shocking and disgraceful thing. My case now was that the accused was only beating, punishing, his wife, until the extreme provocation of being stripped by his mother-in-law had driven him to murder, or alternatively had made him temporarily insane and incapable of knowing what he was doing. If the alternative point had succeeded the prisoner would have been acquitted. Neither point would have succeeded before a professional judge. The Provincial Commissioner, glad to clutch at any straw to avoid sentencing the man to death, convicted him of manslaughter.

After the case, the Provincial Commissioner who, I think, still had me on his conscience, was generous. 'Damn it!' he said, 'I did not know that piece of tribal lore myself, and would not have believed it if you had not called the elders as expert witnesses.' I was sorry when, a few months later, he was transferred as Senior Provincial Commissioner on the Copperbelt, a very tough mining province. I was sorrier still when, a few years later, there was a riot of African mineworkers in which some were shot. The fault, if fault there was, lay with the army but the central Government made the Provincial Commissioner the scapegoat for it. It broke his heart. He retired, and not long afterwards died of a heart attack.

Soon after the Provincial Commissioner left Kasama, I had to crate my household effects once more—I was getting used to that—and bump along in a lorry over two hundred miles of a new earth track to Fort Rosebery. The last man to be posted there had had to walk to it with sixty carriers. I was to assist him as District Officer for a few months until I went on leave, and to take over the District when I came back, though I did not know that at the time I first went there.

Fort Rosebery was an unhealthy station, as its little cemetery revealed, and a queer one. The District was said to be a troublesome one; Districts bordering on a foreign territory usually are. The tribal areas often overflow the international boundaries from both sides so that the worst elements from either side can nip across the border and be sheltered by their blood brothers.

Fort Rosebery bordered the Belgian Congo. Informal agreements were rather easier to make with Belgian administrators than with our Portuguese neighbours bordering other parts of the Protectorate. The Portuguese tended to stand on their dignity and their ancient grandeur.

We had a little arrangement of splendid illegality with the Chef de Poste across the Luapula River. The main agreement assisted us both to uphold the law and minor sub-clauses were added to it as need arose. I was out in his launch with him one day when he shot a hippo which was nearer my side of the river than his.

'Good shot,' I said, 'but it's my hippo and I doubt if you possess a Northern Rhodesia Game licence.'

'Let us' he suggested, 'make a bilateral agreement that for citizens of both our countries the river should be a free zone for hunting and fishing.'

I assented.

The Fort Rosebery station was a centre of white civilization. There was a medical officer and his wife who lived in the haunted house next to mine. A former occupant had committed suicide in it and there were moanings in the roof. There were, incredibly, two teetotal Scottish traders and, credibly, a family of teetotal missionaries across a wooden-bridged small river down the hill. They belonged to a spartan sect called the Plymouth Brethren and regarded smoking and drinking as certain ways to hell. Some distance to the North there was a Catholic Mission. The fathers did good work but threatened their polygamous parishioners with eternal purgatory unless they reduced their establishments to one wife. They tried to persuade me to back them up.

Still further North there was an Anglican Mission of celibate priests who were not on the best of terms with each other. They had been upset by the recent arrival of a middle-aged lady educationist and contended with each other for the duty of sleeping across her threshold in order, so rumour had it, to prevent any of those off duty from attempting ingress.

All this made social entertainment rather tricky. Whenever I held a sundowner party I would, in deference to the Plymouth Brethren, refrain from smoking and serve tea to them and lime juice to the disappointed Catholics, who enjoyed stronger drink and were in need of it: sacramental wine was duty free and they had been importing it in barrels, barrel loads so numerous that they had aroused the curiosity of the Customs Department, which put its foot down.

I also drank lime juice, which gin does not discolour, and made occasional sorties into the kitchen to top up.

They would have been dull parties but for the boy wonder of the Temple Choir Ernest Lough, whose recordings I possessed and always enjoyed. They came in very handy on these occasions, and earned me unaccustomed, almost reverent, esteem from the Plymouth Brethren. 'Hear My Prayer' and 'Oh, for the Wings of a Dove' were their favourites.

But in the main the European population did not much concern me. My work was with the tribesmen. There were four tribes, one of which was unusually wild. The District was riddled with witchcraft. The Banyama—evil spirits in human form who carry off children and devour them—were active in one area. Their existence in the imagination of the villagers was due, I think, to the removal of several freshly buried corpses from their graves by starving old women, during a local famine, coupled with the occasional inevitable tragedy of a child getting lost in the bush and being eaten by lions or other carnivores.

Witchcraft was extremely difficult to deal with. Slavery, fortunately, was not. I was astonished to find that it still existed, even in a small way, and when two old men came to the Boma and complained that they were the slaves of a local chief who was treating them badly, I was furious. No Roman formalities accompanied *their* emancipation. I sent off a Messenger to bring the chief in at once. He sat on the office floor with his two slaves while I told them they were now free men and need not fear any retribution from their former master, as they would realize if they listened to what I was now going to say to him. I told the chief that any other slaves in his or any other chiefdom must be sent in to the Boma, with their owners, and freed. He or any other chief who disobeyed this order would be removed from office by the Governor, lose his government subsidy and see the inside of the Fort Rosebery gaol. I then sent Messengers round the District to investigate. In the event there were only a few old men and women slaves left, relics of tribal wars before the *Pax Britannica*. I need not have got so angry about it anyway. I don't think they really minded being slaves so long as they were well treated. They probably carried on much as before but at least they knew that if they were ill treated a word to me would produce a rapid remedy.

After declaring the abolition of slavery, I was reminded, rather dramatically, of the evils of witchcraft. I went off on a village to village tour of one of the tribal areas, accompanied by a kapasu—a tribal policeman on the staff of a chief. He seemed to be an intelligent man and could read and write a little in the vernacular. One Monday morning he failed to turn up for the day's trek. I asked my Head Messenger to go and tell him to hurry up. 'He is sick,' the Messenger said. 'He cannot come with us any further.'

As we had camped outside a big village on the Sunday and there had been beer-drinking and dancing all day and almost through the night, I was suspicious. I thought he probably had a hangover, and I have two excellent remedies for hangovers. One is to go swimming in rough and icy water, and the other is to sweat it out on a long march in the hot sun. I prescribed the second remedy. The Messenger shook his head. 'The kapasu is very sick and will die' he said, in a matter of fact, off-hand way. I could at first get nothing out of the Messenger as to the nature of the kapasu's sickness, but eventually wore him down.

'The man is bewitched' he said.

'By whom?'

'By his cousin, who is away working on the mines. He had been committing adultery with his cousin's wife, here in this village where they both live, and his cousin has got to hear of it and has written him a letter, bewitching him. Another kapasu brought the village mail from the Boma yesterday, including this letter.'

'Let us' I said, 'go and unbewitch this kapasu. I never heard such nonsense, and I want to see this letter.'

The man was lying on his sleeping mat in his hut, looking remarkably miserable, but otherwise there seemed to be nothing wrong with him. His temperature and pulse were normal, as was his breathing, and he had no pains. He was reluctant to talk but did produce the letter from his pocket. It was in badly spelled and clumsily written Chibemba but the message was simple; I had no difficulty in translating it. All it said was 'I curse you. You are sleeping with my wife while I work here. I curse you. I have bewitched you and you will die.'

The kapasu—a guilty conscience may have helped—was quite certain he was going to die. He would neither eat nor drink but apparently proposed to lie where he was until he died.

I should probably have dealt roughly with him, forcing him to come on with us, making him eat and drink and reasoning with him for hours on end, keeping him active and generally harassed for the first two or three days of the spell, so that he might give up the idea of dying in the hope of getting a little peace and begin to doubt the power of the spell.

'The man who wrote the letter' I said to the Messenger, 'can hardly be a witchdoctor or he would not be away working on the mines.'

'There are plenty of witchdoctors there,' he answered, 'and if this man is not one, he would have paid another to cast the death spell.'

I should have known that after several days of morbid contemplation on his bed nothing could shake the kapasu out of his fate.

But this was my first experience of this kind and I could not believe that the man would just let himself die of what I have heard one doctor call 'melancholia'. What the cause of death is I know not, but a bewitched man can die more quickly than mere hunger and thirst would allow for.

I broke camp and went on my way after a talk with the village headman, whom I told to make the kapasu eat and drink by force if he kept the performance up for more than a day or two. I said I would send a Messenger back at the end of my tour to see that these instructions had been carried out and that the kapasu had not been neglected.

Ten days later I sent a Messenger to the village. The kapasu was dead and buried. The headman had made no attempt to carry out my instructions. 'How could he?' asked the Messenger. 'To have done so could have brought the spell on to himself.'

The next wizardry that I encountered in Fort Rosebery was of a happier kind. The wizard came to my office to report his presence and explain it. There appeared to be nothing outstanding or unusual about him in any way, except for his taste in homemade fur hats. He originated from Southern Rhodesia, and had worked for some time on the South African gold mines, until the grave of the greatest Chief of all time was revealed to him in a dream. God told him, in his dream, to go and dig into this grave, where he would find an all-powerful medicine which he must administer to all the people of Africa, thus curing them of all ills. His name was Ndhlovu.

The medicine was called 'Muchapi'; the exact location of the grave he must not reveal, said Ndhlovu, but it was somewhere in Natal. He had obeyed God's command and now brought a sack of the medicine for the benefit of the people of my district, Fort Rosebery. He would have liked to be able to give the Muchapi to the people free, but unfortunately his travelling expenses were heavy and so he must ask them to pay for it.

I had been forewarned about Ndhlovu by the Native Affairs Department in Lusaka. The racial climate of South Africa and Southern Rhodesia had proved too harsh for him, but in the rather more liberal atmosphere of the Protectorate he had prospered, working his way north from Livingstone and gathering a great following. Native Affairs referred to his 'Muchapi Movement', which in a way it was. The official line was to attempt to discourage the movement by persuading the chiefs against it, but not to attempt to crush it by sterner measures. This was as wise as the suggested discouragement was impracticable. Ndhlovu and his Muchapi medicine swept the country like a bushfire until it burnt itself out. The medicine was nothing more than reddish dust from the roads, but it drove out fear of witchcraft from many people, for a time. As for persuading the chiefs to discourage the 'Muchapi Movement', whenever a chief came to the Boma on some business, I delivered a suitable little lecture on the subject and he said, 'Yes, Bwana,' and departed. Ndhlovu's salesmanship was unusual. He would first of all tour a group of villages (having bribed or persuaded their chief to agree), spinning his yarn about the origin of the medicine and convincing people that if they swallowed a little of it they would henceforth be safe from all evils—on one condition. This was that they must throw away all their fetishes, charms, and other prophylactics against evil spirits and rely solely on the spirit of 'Muchapi'. This kind of condition seems to have appealed to people throughout history—there can only be one supreme Power and to obtain its protection all lesser gods must be abandoned. It certainly appealed to the villagers, who gathered at the crosspaths in their thousands, waiting for Ndhlovu on his second round, and threw their charms and amulets and medicine horns and so on down before him and bought their pinch of Muchapi.

They were buying protection, not only from famine and sickness and the ordinary hazards of life—all of which were due to disgruntled spirits of one kind or another—but from the frightful dangers of witchcraft, the ilombe snake, the kaloloshi and other death-dealing invisible 'familiars' that the witchdoctors might direct to destroy them in their sleep. It would have been an unwise District Commissioner who dared to burst in on such a gathering and arrest Ndhlovu, denying the people the ecstasy of relief from their darkest fears. A charge of obtaining money by false pretences might have been brought against him, but he could not have been prosecuted under the Witchcraft Ordinance. He himself claimed no supernatural powers; the powers were those of the greatest Chief of all time, and resided in the Muchapi taken from his grave. In fact the Muchapi Movement, while it lasted, did much good by lightening fear, and to have attempted to suppress it could easily have driven its fanatical supporters to a bloody uprising.

I wished Ndhlovu had stayed in the district forever, though the witchdoctors would probably have killed him if he had stayed very long. They hated him. But he moved on, into the Congo, having made his little pile, and as the witchdoctors moved back into practice he and his Muchapi were discredited and forgotten.

Fort Rosebery was my first command as District Commissioner —I could hardly have been anything else as there was no other administrator on the station. I enjoyed it, except for occasional attacks of malaria and a succession of sore throats. The doctor peered interestedly down my throat and said, 'Your uvula is elongated and is irritating the back of your throat. I'll cut it short. Ordinary scissors will do. I haven't got the proper instrument. It won't hurt.'

It hurt like hell and I protested.

'That's strange,' he said. 'I cut off hundreds of uvulas in Somaliland and the natives didn't complain.'

The district was not a difficult one, despite its reputation, except for the Batwa, who according to legend had webbed feet, but in fact had not. They were a very primitive tribe of unknown origin who lived in or near the swamps leading to the great Lake Bangweulu. They were short, plump men with hooked noses, and looked like small black Jews. They were a pigmoid tribe who had somehow become detached and isolated. I feel sure that they had a strain of Arab blood in them, introduced by early Arab slavers. Many of them had never seen a white man and few white men had seen any of them. They lived primarily by fishing. Some hunted, using poisoned arrows. The women collected edible wild fruits and tubers but cultivated very little. Nevertheless, the Batwa made a good living by African standards of the time, selling and bartering fish to the peasant tribes. Hardly any of their villages were mapped and there was no sense in mapping them as they were only temporary shacks of reeds and grass on the edge of open water. When the fish moved their feeding grounds so did the Batwa. Their area was rarely toured, as the tax register revealed. There were few names on it and those that were had not paid up so I thought I would go and have a look at them.

It was at the height of the dry season and the water had receded from the first Batwa villages I found. The swamp was some miles ahead. There were very few men about but before I pushed on, having collected hardly any tax, I took several as extra carriers and put them at the head of the file with the Head Messenger to guide us to the swamp villages. The rest of the carriers, now with lighter loads—which I knew would not feel much lighter once we started sloshing through the swamps—were pleased to have the Batwa with them. They found the Batwa dialect hard to understand, but managed to communicate, rather hilariously, with them.

The Batwa walk with a high-stepping action, rather like drum majorettes, owing to the fact that they are accustomed to walking through swamp. Their cheerfulness vanished when they discovered that the carriers behind them were imitating their high stepping and laughing at them instead of with them.

They dropped their loads, turned and raised their spears threateningly, looking very fierce. I intervened hastily, silencing the jokers and restoring peace. But when we reached the last dry village, the Batwa complained that their thighs were becoming chafed as they were not used to walking long distances. I thought this was probably true and sent them back home. Their departure made it more difficult to find the villages when we entered the swamp. We discovered a few . . . but where were the men?

'Gone fishing,' said the women.

'When will they be back?'

The women shrugged.

The Head Messenger said he thought some men were hiding, as there were still some canoes in the channels.

I set off in a canoe with two Messengers. We found fishing camps with fish drying in the sun and fish being smoked over freshly-tended fires. We occasionally saw a canoe, but it always saw us first and disappeared through the reeds. Everywhere the Batwa just melted away before us. They were not in favour of taxation. I decided not to bother about them and set off on the long trek back to the Boma, where there were several construction works going on that needed my supervision, such as it was.

Administrators had to be Jacks-of-all-trades. They might be masters of none but roads, bridges, schools, dispensaries and so on had to be constructed, and as there was nobody else available in the rural areas it was the administrators who had to construct them. In fact, apart from doing the tricky jobs like marking out foundations or surveying the line of a road, much of the credit for these developments should go to the African labourers and a sprinkling of rough carpenters and bricklayers, trained by missionaries.

My civil engineering apprenticeship under Tom Chicken at Serenje had covered roads and bridges, fortunately, for I now had to make a road from Fort Rosebery to the Congo border and put up a wooden bridge *en route*, and a few culverts besides.

Roads were easy enough, so long as you did not try to keep them straight and dodged rock outcrops and other obstacles. Trees had to be chopped down, their stumps excavated and the holes filled in and rammed down with hardwood stampers. Then earth, or gravel (if any), was piled on and shaped to give a camber to each side of the road. The camber, the side drains, and the herringbone drains leading out of them, were the real secrets of roadmaking. Without them, the road would be a river of mud in the rainy season.

Culverts were also needed to carry off flood water at the lowest points where the road undulated. Sighting them by eye, I had discovered, was unreliable. They were always just one side or the other of the bottom of the undulation and the floodwater found its own level and swamped the road. A forty-four-gallon drum of water rolled to the approximate site in the dry season and tipped out onto the road solved the problem. The culvert was sited where the puddle remained.

Bridges were more difficult than roads, but looked more impressive—until they were washed away. My first bridge, across the Kaombe River, built in the Serenje District following Tom's assurance that any fool could build a bridge, had taught me a valuable lesson in man management. If you have to do something that neither you nor anyone available knows how to do, tell your most promising subordinate to do it. Then walk away quickly before he can argue and stay away until he has done it.

I had stood on the bank of the river at the appointed spot and instructed my senior messenger to build the bridge. The Messenger had replied apologetically that he did not know how to build a bridge. 'Any fool can build a bridge,' I had countered walking quickly away. Neither of us had known that Tom, relenting, had sent the Boma carpenter after us. Upon his arrival the Messenger had immediately passed the buck. 'You are to build a bridge, over there.'

The carpenter had looked at the ravine, shaken his head and attempted to lick his elbows, to indicate the impossibility of the task. 'Chairs and tables I can make,' he had replied, 'but bridges, no. And over that . . . ?'

'The Bwana says,' the Messenger had replied loftily as he walked away, 'that any fool can build a bridge.'

The carpenter had built the bridge without anything other than what the forest provided—barring the carriers' axe blades, which were made by a native smith. Hardwood pegs substituted for nails, and lusisi for wire. Whenever I had insisted that a heavier tree trunk should be used in place of a lighter one it had stayed in position just long enough to disprove the carpenter's assertion that it would not, and then crashed down into the ravine.

I had learned from that bridge and the one I now had to build did not worry me. What *did* worry me was the instruction I had received to build an aerodrome at Fort Rosebery. A small party of visiting experts had selected the site on paper. There were no aircraft to use it but apparently the development of air communications was being planned. The first thing to do was to level the ground. As soon as I arrived back from tour I clumped off through the bush to examine the site, which was a rough sea of anthills. An average termite anthill is about ten feet high and thirty feet in diameter. It is extremely difficult to shift with a pick and shovel since the earth is bound tight and hard by the ants' secretion. It cannot be blown up by an amateur using the simple method of tunnelling under it, pushing a stick of gelignite into the tunnel, lighting the fuse and running away, for within it and far beneath and around its base there is a maze of ant tunnels and excavations which absorb the shock, so that the anthill lifts indignantly an inch or two in a cloud of dust and settles down again, sullen and immovable as ever. Experts using many small charges and a maze of wires are reputedly able to blow anthills to pieces but it must be very risky. Blowing things up is always risky and I prefer one big bang when I have no need to count, nor to wonder if I have counted wrongly and left any smouldering, unexploded, charges to walk into.

In the event, the airfield was never completed. After the area had been stumped of trees, a hundred labourers—forty with picks, forty with shovels, and twenty with wheelbarrows—battled on for several months, until another expert from the capital city arrived and proclaimed the site unsuitable. The villagers were delighted and moved on to the stumped land, burned the felled trees for ash fertilizer, and grew some bumper crops on it.

I was delighted too. There was still some money unspent under my expenditure warrant for levelling the aerodrome runway, and I could put it to good use. The outbuildings on the Fort Rosebery station were quite inadequate to house all the stores and implements and impedimenta with which an outstation is cluttered, so I built a large burnt-brick and iron-roofed shed.

Soon after the shed was completed, two District Officers arrived at the Boma in a lorry piled up with their household effects, on transfer to Fort Rosebery. It seemed odd to me that my one-man station was suddenly to become a three-man station and odder still that Provincial Headquarters had not advised me of this.

The older of the two, a middle-aged man, was to take over the District; I and the other, who was about my age, would be working under him. I said I did not think much of this arrangement. The new D.C. grinned amiably and said, 'You know how it is: they like playing with their pins at headquarters.'

So I showed the new arrivals round the station. Both were apparently keen on playing squash racquets. I took some modest pride in showing them my new shed. The D.C. paced it out, thoughtfully. 'It only needs plastering inside,' he said. 'It will do fine for a squash court.'

That evening the three of us took a walk along the river that ran through the station. It was shallow and fast flowing except for some large deep pools here and there. We stopped at the edge of one of them.

'Good,' said the D.C. 'We can swim here.'

I shook my head and said, 'Crocodiles.'

They both scoffed at that. 'It's not a big enough river for crocs,' the D.C. asserted.

So they both swam every evening for the next few days until I shot an eleven-foot crocodile early one morning, as it lay basking in the early rays of the sun on the edge of one of the pools. They then decided to concentrate on squash and busied themselves with my shed.

I never saw the completion of its conversion, but I soon understood the reason why my one-man station had suddenly had its number increased. A letter arrived from the Secretary for Native Affairs, telling me that I was transferred to Broken Hill, a town on the railway line.

CHAPTER TEN

The Line of Rail

I NEVER SERVED on an outstation again. Perhaps that was just as well. I was looking upon the natives as a sort of Rousseau product, only a good deal rougher: children of Nature who had not felt, and never would feel, the impact of western civilization, who were content to stay as they were, with the security of peace and justice guaranteed by the Boma. At that time, as far as the remote rural areas were concerned, I was not far wrong in this belief. But in the towns and the white settled areas, the picture was different.

Broken Hill was a mining town and the centre of a rural district including a European farming belt as well as the tribal areas. I arrived there in June 1936 and stayed there for nearly four years, with a home leave in between, feeling very smug. I had passed my Bar examinations and, previously, my Colonial Service Law examination with distinction, thanks to a ruse which I had always employed in examinations, even at school. By this method you seek, far outside the range of the set books, a scholarly volume normally studied only by professors, find two or three passages in it which you can actually understand, learn them by heart, and somehow drag at least one of them into the answer to a question, quoting the authority. This impresses the examiners with your fascination for the subject and the breadth of your reading.

I had also passed the Higher Language examination owing to being set the wrong papers. My language was Chibisa. I found the papers extraordinarily difficult, and having dealt with them as best I could, took them to the invigilator, the missionary who had set the papers, and complained. He was quite shaken.

'This examination is for Chilamba students' he said. 'Who sent you here?'

'The Secretary for Native Affairs' I replied.

'I must write to him about it.'

'So must I' I said.

We both did. I had no reply and I doubt if the missionary did, though I never saw him again (he was sent off on transfer to another mission) but the Secretary covered up cleverly by gazetting me as having passed—in Chibemba. I did not think it wise to tell him once more that Chibisa was my language, neither then nor later, when he detailed me to undertake the oral part of the Chibemba exam for a lady in the African Education Department. Happily, two examiners were always required for an oral examination and my colleague really knew Chibemba.

After it was over he said, 'She's no good at all. Don't you agree? We'll have to fail her, I'm afraid.' I concurred.

Success in all these examinations, I felt, must have sufficiently impressed Authority for me to be sent to Broken Hill as Resident Magistrate of a Class I Court and also to take over the District from the D.C. who was due for leave.

The facts were, it transpired, that the Chief Justice was agitating for more Resident Magistrates, who had to be qualified lawyers. The Secretary for Native Affairs was insisting that no more of his administrators, lawyers or not, could be spared for other departments. The British gift for compromise resulted in my being seconded to and working for the Judiciary, while remaining in and working for the Administration. The fact that I was not a qualified barrister and would not be until I had kept more terms at Lincoln's Inn and spent six months of pupillage in chambers, was ignored. The Colonial Service had no time for splitting hairs.

The Resident Magistrate's circuit covered four towns strung out down the railway line over a distance of about three hundred miles. The importance that even justice attaches to money was reflected in my judicial powers. I could try all criminal cases except murder and rape—both in theory punishable by death, although rape never was in practice. I could even try a capital case, under delegated powers, if the Chief Justice could not get round to it. He was the sole High Court Judge and the only Judge of Appeal, but a Puisne Judge was soon appointed. True, any sentence I imposed of over two years' imprisonment was subject to confirmation by the High Court after examination of the case record, and the Chief Justice could make a random check by calling for the record of a case from my monthly return list of cases heard, which he occasionally did. My powers in civil cases, however, were limited to causes which did not involve a claim exceeding £100.

There was a real Court at Broken Hill, with a wooden dock and a witness box. On a dais was the magistrate's bench, a deal table covered with green baize, on which a cast iron paperweight rested.

The D.C., who showed me round the station, led me through a door onto the dais. 'This' he said 'is the Court.' He then paused, looked down at the red-oxided, polished, cement floor, picked up the paperweight and threw it at the floor. I made no comment. We all have our little eccentricities.

'A bloody great cobra, can't you see it?' he said.

And so it was, copper coloured, rearing up and with a strong dislike for paperweights, even when they missed. But on the polished floor its belly scales could get little grip and it was easily killed by a Messenger with a long broom.

The General Manager of the Broken Hill Mine, a hard-bitten but decent American, called on me. He seemed to be looking at me rather curiously when we were chatting and finally said 'You're very young for the job.'

He might have been even more worried about my inexperience had he known that he would soon be in the dock on a manslaughter charge. He declined to engage a counsel for his defence, commenting that all lawyers were liars, and I had to do a great deal of research to find a leading case on which to acquit him. The stupidity of the Mining Ordinance, later altered, made the Manager directly responsible in law for any accident on the mine. A cage had been lowered too far in the sump of a shaft where a white miner was working, and had killed him. The Manager could not possibly be blamed and fortunately I dug up a sound precedent for not blaming him—at least, I hope it was sound.

I may not have known much about law, but from service on four outstations I had learned something about the natives who came to work in the towns, and it seemed to me that some changes in the past practice of the courts that were now mine, were needed. Far too many petty offences were brought up, sometimes on admissions of guilt with the standard fine attached. Most of the offenders appeared in person and pleaded guilty to being found without a pass of some sort, or to riding a bicycle on the wrong side of the street or without a lamp, or to being in breach of one of a dozen or more township regulations. Perhaps twenty of such cases, each morning, would take about as many minutes of my time to get through. Some of the offenders, I thought, probably had no idea of why they were in the dock. A five shilling or two-and-sixpenny fine to a man earning from five to ten shillings a week, or a few days imprisonment in default, was, I thought, too much. I cut the fines down to a shilling and began demanding police evidence on about one case in five. This gave the Police Prosecutor, who brought the cases rightly enough in accordance with his duty, a great deal of trouble. Occasionally he could produce no evidence because the arresting constable was out on patrol, and sometimes the accused had a reasonable defence, once it was dragged out of him.

Soon the number of these petty cases dropped considerably, but I was still depressed with the knowledge that a raw villager labouring for a time in the town did not understand that he must ride his cycle on the left of the road, that he must not piddle discreetly against a tree, and that various other things which he could do in his village he could not do in a town. So I wrote a little book about it all, in basic English, also explaining the mysteries of court procedure and the rights of the accused person. Very few Africans could read English and not so many more could read at all, but the Government made a digest of the book and had it printed in the main vernaculars to be enclosed with every Identity Certificate issued, so I suppose it was of some help.

Another cause for depression was the discovery that some of the white men in the towns were by no means like the missionaries and civil servants and occasional traders that I had met on outstations. There were some very nasty specimens indeed. There was the lady who had one of her employees tied to a tree on suspicion of theft and prodded his chest with a lighted cigarette in an effort to obtain a confession. There was a more amusing, and possibly mentally retarded matron, who enquired of a colleague who dealt with licensing whether she could have a licence to open a brothel. He told her that no such licence existed, and enquired curiously where she would find the staff for such an establishment.

'Well, there's my two daughters' she replied.

In general, the white population seemed to think that the law should be applied more favourably to them than to those with darker skins. My popularity with many of them was not high when they realized that I did not share this view, though they never threatened to tar and feather me as they threatened the Resident Magistrate further north, on the Copperbelt. He had warned a European youth whom he had twice convicted of brutally assaulting an African, that if he were convicted again for a similar offence he would be sentenced to strokes with the cane. The youth was again convicted, and caned. The rumpus amongst the whites was such that the Governor felt it necessary to go up and investigate and later an official enquiry was held into the affair, which should of course have been ignored. The police would have dealt with the white miners had they dared to attempt to carry out their threat.

In criminal cases it was seldom difficult, after listening to a mass of evidence, to decide whether a man was guilty or not. Every lawyer knows that ninety-five per cent of cases are decided on fact, not points of law. The real worry for a Magistrate was to decide what sentence to impose in the best interests of society and of the offender, for every offender is an individual. Clemency may show a profit from one man and a loss from another. My major objective was to stop a first offender becoming a second.

An elderly but powerful Afrikaner farmer, with a wooden leg from the knee, stumped into the dock one morning and pleaded guilty to stealing six wheelbarrows from the mine. He had retired from the mine a year before and taken up a piece of land and needed some wheelbarrows for his labourers. So he drove into the mine one night and loaded up the wheelbarrows. He had thought they would never be missed; the mine had hundreds of wheelbarrows.

He was very apologetic and ashamed of having been caught and of appearing in the dock. I sentenced him to a fine of £50 and the necessary formal one-day imprisonment, which meant that he did not go to prison but was discharged at the rising of the Court. He was far from rich and I knew that losing £50 would give him a nasty knock. I made no comment on his behaviour. I did not believe in castigating a convicted prisoner in court, on his 'deplorable character' or 'vicious conduct', for it always seemed to me that the prisoner would regard the few simple words of the sentence itself, such as 'six months hard labour', as sufficient criticism. This man was not a criminal type in any case. Miners often helped themselves to a useful tool, but he had gone a little too far. He was a simple-minded sort and had lost his leg through walking straight into a trap he had set for wild pig.

The Flag-Wagger

Some of my methods and decisions might seem strange to London magistrates, but my circumstances were not theirs. We had no probation officers, no court missionaries, no reformatories. There was no provision in the law for suspended sentences and no Prisoners Aid Society, and when it came to sentencing a young African on a conviction for a crime that was more than trivial, it was often difficult to decide what to do with him. If he had come into town from his village to seek work he would have no money, so it would be useless to fine him; he would have to go to gaol on default of payment and unless he was a hardened criminal this was undesirable. If his father could be contacted I could see if he had any money to pay a fine for his son. If he had he could, and always would, pay the son's fine and take it out of the youth afterwards. But his father might be a hundred miles away in his village. I often therefore decided, if I thought the young criminal needed a sharp lesson, to sentence him to a few cuts with the cane, until the false sentimentality of politicians in Westminster, through pressure on the Colonial Office, practically put an end to the use of the cane, with the result that there were more youngsters in prisons learning the arts of crime from the old lags than there had been previously.

My most appalling duty, as Under-Sheriff—the office was combined with that of Resident Magistrate—was to witness hangings, conduct the brief inquest on the executed man, and certify that death was due to a broken neck. This duty was necessary in order to ensure that the condemned man should not suffer death by strangulation instead of the instantaneous and painless death of a broken neck. The Under-Sheriff had to check everything the evening before, the weight of the man, length of rope, stretch of rope, action of the leather-bound loop, to make sure that nothing could go wrong and cause unnecessary suffering. The British practice was meticulously followed.

On the rare occasions when this duty was imposed on me, I would awake after bad dreams—in one I was standing over an ant hole from which hundreds of ants were emerging and I had to kill every one before it got away—and drive to the prison at dawn. The Medical Officer, who also had to be in attendance, always offered me a brandy, which I refused. With the nausea already in my throat I would have brought the brandy up immediately. I also felt that if this was my duty I must perform it without assistance.

The Line of Rail

I only saw one man hanged that I had no pity for. He was a killer, wanted for previous murders and convicted of a most brutal murder and robbery. Most of the others, brutal and savage though they may have been, I would have liked to have seen have their sentences reduced by royal prerogative to life imprisonment. There was nearly always drink or passion or superstition involved in their crimes, though not to the extent of legal excuse.

The Royal Prerogative of pardon was exercised by the Governor, as the King's representative. As self-government developed, he invited the opinions of his Executive Councillors, but was not bound by them, though in practice he rarely, if ever, went against a majority opinion.

Many years later, as a Minister on Executive Council, I invariably based my own advice both on whether the murder was committed for personal gain and on whether the murderer, from his past record and the reports of experts, appeared to be a killer type from whom the public including his fellow prisoners and the warders, should be protected.

Superstition or religion—the two were perhaps inseparable—often provided the motive for the most gruesome and cold-blooded killings. African religion rests in the belief in the power of the dead, of the family spirits, and the tribal spirits. They must accordingly be propitiated, avenged, or their wishes obeyed, in accordance with religious rules and rituals. Two specific cases of religiously inspired killings give some idea of the demands which the spirits may make upon their living descendants. Only the second required an opinion from me in Executive Council; the first was before my time.

A European trader was ambushed and speared to death in the Kasempa District, while cycling home from one of his village stores. He might have been carrying money, he might have been cheating the people in his buying of skins and selling of goods, he might have had an unsavoury reputation for abducting village girls; all the likely motives were at first suspected. African detectives and police informers were scattered around the area and loose talk led to the arrest of the murderers. Their case was this. A labour recruiter for the Johannesburg gold mines had recruited a number of men from the district a year before. Some of them had died while working on the mine to which they were sent, from what cause was not made known. There may have been an outbreak of smallpox or typhus or they may have died from pneumonia which in those days, before the sulphonamides, took heavy toll of workers from tropical areas in the bitter Johannesburg winter. But as far as the Kaonde tribesmen of the Kasempa district were concerned, the spirits were angry at the deaths of their relatives who could not, from so far away, join them in their local spiritual abode. The recruiter was to blame, and the witchdoctors had divined that the spirits would only be appeased by his death. He would be round again soon and must be killed. The recruiter never did come round again, and this was awkward. He was a big man, red-haired and with a red beard. The local trader was also a big man with blond hair and beard. The witchdoctors, after consultation with the spirits, announced that the trader would do instead of the recruiter. And so he did. The villagers ambushed him and speared him to death.

The second case was of a kind quite new to me and I think peculiar to the tribe concerned. A man had died in circumstances which would have appeared normal enough to most people, but did not so appear to some of his relatives, who suspected witchcraft. At the funeral, as the coffin neared the grave, it became quite uncontrollable and kept hitting a woman who was amongst the mourners, finally bashing her to death against a tree. The pallbearers were quite unable to stop the spirit of the dead man in the coffin from revenge on the witch who had caused his death. Naturally this evidence did not impress a British judge, and the pallbearers were sentenced to life imprisonment. In the circumstances it would only need one pallbearer, suspecting the woman, to manoeuvre the coffin to strike her once to convince the others that the dead man's spirit was at work and they must follow it. Even an accident, a pallbearer stumbling and the coffin hitting the woman, could have been sufficient sign for the bearers to imagine that they felt the directions of the spirit and must carry them out.

Happily, I never had to try anybody for murder and a good deal of my work did not involve punishing anybody for anything. On outstations, I had become used to Africans bringing their troubles to me, but now, in the towns, some of the white people seemed to regard me as a sort of universal aunt. Away from the towns, my office door had always been open, and I saw no reason to keep it closed at Broken Hill. I told my secretary and my Court clerk that anyone who wished to see me must be let pass without interrogation, for a man who has just summoned up enough courage to open his heart is easily put off.

Dealing with these human problems was a relief from sitting on the bench, from which position one sees the worst side of life, so that after a time the abnormal begins to appear as normal. The world then seems to be mostly populated with criminals, lying witnesses, avaricious plaintiffs and dishonest defendants.

The rate of European crime—as opposed to petty offences—was, by Western standards, low, although no lower, in proportion to the white population, than the rate of African crime. I never liked to see a white man in the dock, not because I had any special sympathy with him but because I thought he set a bad example to the Africans and in general I had more sympathy for African criminals than for their European counterparts, who were comparatively affluent, knew the law and had little excuse for breaking it.

The factors leading Africans into crime were complex and in some ways unique. The adventurous young man of the village could no longer prove his manhood and attract the prettiest girl to be his wife by blooding his spear in a tribal war. Instead, he could set off on the long trek to the white men's towns, brave the hazards of strange laws and customs, and work adventurously underground or among clanking trucks and hissing railway engines. He hoped to return after a year or two with a bicycle, gramophone, blankets and presents for the family. The hero would also bring back a dress or two for his betrothed and some money for the brideprice.

He might succeed in his adventure, or he might not. If he failed to find work, the prospect of returning to his village as a failure was too humiliating to contemplate. He could not starve in the town. There would certainly be members of his own tribe somewhere about who were in duty bound to feed him from what little they had themselves. But he would sometimes be hungry and always poor. Unemployed and away from the sanctions of his village and tribal society, his behaviour could easily deteriorate. Stealing from rich white foreigners or even from natives of another tribe would not concern his home society in any event. And burglary or housebreaking requires courage and is adventurous. A sense of guilt or shame would not depress him. Discovery in crime would not matter greatly, since he would be well fed in prison and prison was the white man's institution. There was little shame attached to being one of its inmates for a time.

He might reach the same decisions even if he found work, regular or occasional. In the detribalised polyglot society of the town there were plenty of card sharps, harlots and shebeen-keepers to relieve him of his small earnings. The more adventurous and courageous he was, indeed the more imaginative and capable, the more he would rebel against misfortune.

The criminal career of one youngster particularly interested me. His earlier offences were at my expense, and for a time I was able to keep track of him. His name was, allegedly, Ephraim.

I engaged him as a house servant. He said he knew the work, but he obviously did not. He learned quickly and became the most intelligent, energetic, and capable servant I ever had, cheerful and with a naughty sense of humour. He was also handsome and therefore a great success with the girls and a favourite in the beer-halls. Small articles of value, including my gold cufflinks and dress shirt studs began to disappear. But I might have lost them, or the cook might have taken a fancy to them.

The losses ceased when the police rescued Ephraim from my car which was upside down in the rockery of somebody's garden on a street corner which he had failed to negotiate. He had never driven before, but felt that a little excursion round the town would be interesting and he would bring the car back long before I walked home from the office. What I did not know, would not hurt me.

The police brought various charges against him, and he went to gaol for three months, where he learned his future trade from more experienced felons. Eight or nine months later I saw him at a dance in the African Welfare Hall at Lusaka. I had been asked by the Committee to judge the dancing, modern ballroom-style which the upper strata of African society were just beginning to take to. I was also to present the prizes.

The best couple was soon obvious, a man in a dinner jacket and a girl in a long but very ill-fitting second-hand gown. I could not see their faces clearly in the crowded hall until they passed close to the dais. The man was Ephraim. Nevertheless, he and his partner must have first prize if ballroom justice was to be upheld.

I was flanked by the Committee. 'Where are the prizes?' I asked.

'We have no prizes. It is for the Bwana to give the prizes.'

'But I haven't got any prizes.'

'Money will do' said the Committee graciously.

Ephraim mounted the platform, beaming with pleasure—and wearing my cufflinks and studs in his dress shirt. We shook hands and I gave him a £1 note, but I could not forbear from the sour comment that at last I knew where my links and studs were. He pocketed the £1 and melted away.

I next heard of him from a colleague in another town, who had sentenced him to three years on his record plus a particularly daring burglary. He had entered a house where the owner and his wife were sleeping unusually soundly after a sundown party of extended duration. Before getting drunk himself, Ephraim took the precaution, having switched on the lights, of removing all the empty bottles, half to the back entrance and half to the front, and breaking them up just outside the doors. He then returned and settled down to a private party of his own, before going right through the house, switching on all the lights and filling a mealie sack with the occupants' possessions. He also had a late supper, *en passant*, in the kitchen. The bedroom was his last call, but there the fumes of alcohol and the unaccustomed richness of the food overtook him. He was sick on the floor and lay down at the foot of the bed to sleep.

Later the houseowner awoke, found the light on and sat up to look around. He saw Ephraim, let out a yell which awakened him, and jumped out of bed, losing a second or two to grab a golf club from a corner of the room. Ephraim cleared the broken glass outside the open back door easily. His pursuer did not, and abandoned the chase to attend to his bleeding feet.

Ephraim, I think, may have been an incorrigable criminal, but others were not, sometimes not even the most dangerous ones, like the prisoner who wanted to kill the head gaoler at Broken Hill prison, a very big and powerful man, an ex-army boxer and not easily shaken. Arriving on a routine weekly prison inspection one Saturday morning, I found him much agitated. A small but lithe convict in his early twenties had tried to go for him with an axe, but had been overpowered by other prisoners.

The Flag-Wagger

'He's the most dangerous man I've got—has been ever since he came here,' the gaoler complained.

I looked at the prisoner's record of larceny and house-breaking and several assaults. The man himself seemed a little mad. He might, I thought, have been smoking dagga (cannabis), which periodically found its way into the prison. Or he might be in the highly strung state that some prisoners get into in the last week or so of a longish sentence. He was due out in a few days, but I had to cut his good conduct remission, which kept him in another two or three weeks.

He refused to talk at all, and I said I would see him again later. It seemed to me that if I was going to start a one man Prisoners Aid Society, as I had already decided to do, I might as well choose a tough prisoner to start with.

I had him brought to my office twice during the following week and asked the warders to wait outside while I talked to him. He spoke very freely about himself and his family, his village and so on, and was very unhappy about the life he had got into.

I said I would try to get him a job. He shook his head. 'I can't work for Europeans' he said. 'I'm very quick-tempered and when they shout at me I get too angry.'

What he wanted to do, it seemed, was to mend bicycles. Since the state of government bicycles is always deplorable on any station, I managed to feed him bicycles until his release, and he mended them very well in prison.

I thought he would want to start a little business of his own in the town, but he had no such wish. His village was in a well populated area where there were many bicycles, and he wanted to work at home. 'If I stay here I shall steal things' he said casually. I know that he mended bicycles in his village for the next three years. After that I was transferred once again and heard no more of him.

After this encouraging start, I continued to experiment in the rehabilitation of a few selected prisoners—I had no time for more—and as far as I know none of them went back to crime. One, a big fellow of about thirty-five and of commanding presence, obviously wanted a job with a little authority, and a kindly contractor agreed to give him one. Many years later he was still working for the contractor, who told me he was the best *capitao* he had ever had.

My dream as a young man, that in this as in other parts of the Empire (outside the white dominions) we could bring the native peoples up to a reasonable condition of prosperity and civilization in a generation, my generation, was, I now realized, only a pipe dream. Even with unlimited money and staff this task would have taken the Colonial Service, as it will take the young African governments of today, much longer than that. But there were small things that one could do to add some brightness to life in the towns, where the African population was concentrated, instead of being scattered over the unrewarding soil of the bush at a density of six to the square mile. Film shows were one possibility.

There was only one cinema, in the Mine Club, for Europeans only. The operator was a good chap. He said there was an old broken down projector for silent films somewhere on the mine. He might be able to make it work if I could get hold of it.

The Mine Manager gave it to me and it was pressed into service. There was a field at the back of the Boma offices which with the aid of some rough carpentry and whitewashed calico to make a screen, I turned into an open air cinema, admission free. I have forgotten where the antique films came from, but I think we found a stack of them somewhere on the mine. They were mostly Charlie Chaplins and Westerns.

The Africans flocked to the show, every Saturday evening. It had to end before nine owing to the stupid night pass system. (In effect this was a curfew for Africans except for anyone who carried a note from his employer giving him permission to be out later on a specific night for a specific purpose. Any really intelligent and careful burglar carried one, forged by an African clerk or schoolboy, against the unlikely event of being stopped by a white police officer. The African police on night duty were mostly illiterate.) The Chaplin films made the people laugh until they cried. They understood every wordless word of his expressions and gestures and clowning. They bellowed for Charlie before the show started. They shouted 'Charlie, Charlie' whenever they had enough breath left from laughing, and they called for more when the film ended.

The Westerns puzzled them a little at first. They could understand the painted warriors fighting the white men and being shot down, but they could not understand why the white men often shot each other. However, they soon came to recognize the villains and the heroes and backed the hero to the hilt, shouting warnings to him as occasion demanded.

Breakdowns in the performances, scratched films and erratic speeds were all accepted cheerfully by the audience. When we had exhausted our repertoire of films we showed them again, and then again. And each time the Africans seemed to like them just as much as before. But after a few months the inevitable day came when the projector broke down beyond repair and there was no money to buy another. It was a good many years before the natives of Broken Hill saw a film again, but at least football, by now, had come to stay. (I sometimes wonder if football is not the best thing that the white man brought to Africa.)

The Mine Compound Superintendant had already raised two teams of African mineworkers. They even had football jerseys and a levelled field in which to play each other, having wheedled money from the mining company for these things. We obviously needed more teams and a League and a Championship Cup. I thought it should be easy enough but it turned out to be a little more difficult than I had anticipated. Everything always was.

I called a meeting of respected citizens of the various African communities, railway workers, government employees, township workers and others. They agreed that more football would be 'a very good thing'. In the rather unsuitable surroundings of my court room in which I held meetings of this kind and which was soon to become the boardroom of the Football League's directors, they would probably have agreed that football was 'a bad thing', if that had been my thesis.

They would find out how many young men in each community wanted to play football and choose the teams, which would appoint the captains. 'All right?'

'Yes, Bwana.'

I would find the playing grounds and I could get some old footballs discarded by the European Mine and Railway teams and others, which would do for a start.

'Yes, Bwana. That would be very good.'

'The grounds will have to be scuffled with hoes to clear away any scrub and long grass. But you can tell the young men who want to play football to do that.'

'They may not agree with us, Bwana . . . these young men . . . hoeing is women's work.'

'All right. I'll ask them myself. And they can cut some bush poles for goal posts and strip the bark for lusisi to tie the pole across the top with. And there are other things. Football jerseys and whistles and a Cup.'

'A cup, Bwana?'

I explained the nature and purpose of the Cup and we discussed the possibilities of having a collection in each compound. Boots, fortunately, would not be needed. Nobody could run in boots except the Europeans, who were used to them.

The possibilities of collecting any money appeared to be remote, so I said I would buy the Cup and the players could wear ordinary shirts, but one team must all wear white shirts. The other could play in any shirts they possessed that were not white.

Shirts would get torn and shirts were precious, they said, doubtfully.

'All right. One team can wear any old shirts and the other will wear no shirts, then everybody will know who is on which side.'

That, it seemed, would not be fair. The shirtless team would feel inferior, at a disadvantage. The mine bought the jerseys for their teams, could not the Government pay for jerseys?

'This isn't a Government thing,' I said, without conviction.

On the whole, everything went as well as could be expected. The grounds were no problem. The land was all Crown land and I was the Crown. The young men scuffled the earth clear of obstructions, though the unevenness of the pitches caused the ball to bounce in unexpected directions.

Progress gathered speed. Fixtures were arranged, Vice-Captains and Secretaries and Treasurers were appointed, though none of them performed any duties. I did the paper work and kept the books and refereed, rather unnecessarily, as there was no need to maintain law and order: and so long as everybody is happy the rules of a game are not of much importance. Everybody was happy. By the end of the second season, the League, thank God, was running itself with the aid of several of the more educated fans, and never looked back.

The number of Africans with a full primary school education was very small and there were practically none with secondary education. Very few women had had any formal schooling at all.

The problems of my own African clerks brought home to me the difficulties of this small but growing class, often mockingly referred to by whites as 'the intelligentsia'. They were eager for more education, obtainable only from books, which they could not afford to buy, or by discussion with Europeans—for their wives and relatives were uneducated. Few Europeans were prepared to discuss anything with them.

I lent them books, which they read avidly, and also started a sort of evening class for the discussion of topical subjects, inviting all English-speaking literates to attend if they wished. It was less than a drop of water where an ocean was needed but at least the drop was welcomed. I learned more from the discussions than they did, particularly when I took up a subject that they knew far more about than I did, such as witchdoctors and witchcraft.

The profession of witchdoctoring seemed to me to cover a number of different activities which merged into a sort of spectrum: herbalist, psychologist, spiritualist, hypnotist, diviner, murderer. A witchdoctor who kept to the top part of the spectrum probably did more good than harm.

The law against witchcraft was not very effective and baffled the villagers as much as it did me. The Witchcraft Ordinance provided severe penalties for anybody accusing another of being a 'witch', a term covering both males and females. This was a necessary provision because such an accusation made falsely by some evil-minded villager with a tongue clever enough to convince others often led to the alleged witch being murdered for the 'safety' of the village. It was sometimes made against some unfortunate old man or woman who was perhaps a little mad or unusually shrewish or in general a nuisance to the village and would be no loss to the community. It was hardly ever made against that powerful witch, the real witchdoctor. Few villagers would have the courage to accuse *him*.

Another section of the Ordinance imposed heavy penalties on a person pretending to possess supernatural powers, in other words claiming to be a witch or a witchdoctor. It also proscribed various activities, such as divining, or trial by poison or by boiling water.

The law took the line that people with supernatural powers could not and did not exist. Obviously this line had to be taken but it was impossible to reconcile the Africans to this proposition, which was not even in accord with the teachings of many of the missionaries who tried to convert them to Christianity. The Africans were quite certain that people with supernatural powers for good or evil existed: even a few of those claiming these powers believed that they actually possessed them.

The worst kind of witchdoctor was little more than a freelance assassin. One called Mundina was of this kind. His clients would offer him money or cattle as payment for the elimination of an enemy, a rival, a husband with a coveted wife, a nagging mother-in-law, or a much feared witch—perhaps some innocent old crone suspected of causing the deaths of children, which were in fact due to some little-known disease.

Mundina possessed a Kaloloshi. This is a 'gun' made from a human bone, usually a femur. The witchdoctor points it at the setting sun and says 'So-and-so will die' and the next day 'So-and-so' is dead. The witchdoctor's problem is how to kill the man by natural means without being found out, so that the people will believe that the man has been killed by supernatural power.

Mundina's method was simple. Day after day an African village is practically empty, with the men, women and children—even the babies on their mothers' backs—away in the fields, leaving three or four helplessly old people lying with their bemused memories in the sun or the shade, according to the season. It is easy for anybody either in his own village or staying for a week or so in one of the villages of his area where tribal kinship compels hospitality, to discover on which side of the hut his victim sleeps and at which end is his pillow or headrest. Mundina took great care to locate exactly where the victim's head would be, when he was asleep. He would then make a hole in the wall of the hut through which he could shoot the man or woman through the head. A hut wall is just two or three inches of dried clay held together with a rough lattice of reeds or saplings. The general decrepitude of the huts was such that nobody was likely to notice one more hole, and that very close to the ground. On several occasions Mundina miscalculated, either wounding or missing the victim; and once, he killed the wrong person.

Mundina possessed another weapon, an eighteen-inch length of iron pipe, bent and welded solid at one end for a butt and drilled with a touch-hole. Rammed with a charge of gunpowder and load of shot, it was most effective. He would creep up to the hut at dead of night, push the gun through the hole, and fire. Before the village was roused he would be back on his sleeping mat. The villagers believed that the shot materialized from nowhere, by magic. Certainly, any that doubted this kept quiet, until one day a man who was neither gullible nor terrified spoke up, and in due course Mundina was hanged for murder.

Sometimes an alleged witch or other offender, 'divined' by the witchdoctor, might be given the chance of a trial by boiling water or by *mwavi*, a vegetable poison. If he could plunge his arm into the boiling water and bring it out unscalded, or if he could vomit up the poison quick enough, he was acquitted.

Our discussion group meeting on witchcraft was encouraging. Several men said openly that they did not believe in witchcraft. Then a man handed me a letter addressed to a brother of his, who was not present. 'What would you say about this?' he queried. 'There's witchcraft medicine on it.'

The letter, like the one which had caused the death of the kapasu, was from an aggrieved husband at work on the Copperbelt accusing the addressee of committing adultery with his wife. It ended: 'When you read this you will go blind.'

Scrawled all over the bottom half of the piece of paper were streaks of red and yellow crayon pencil marks, which was the blinding medicine.

I said 'You haven't gone blind and nor have I, from looking at this letter. Has your brother?'

'Not yet' he replied cautiously.

'Let's all look at this rubbish' I suggested. 'We'll pass it round.' There were some doubts about the wisdom of this, but when I had rubbed it over my eyes most of the men were prepared to look at it and laugh at it.

All this rushing about blowing whistles for offsides and winding the handle of an antique cinema projector and holding little soirées on witchcraft may not have been seemly activities for an imperial proconsul, but they improved my understanding: my relationship with the Africans was gradually changing from that of master and servant or ruler and ruled. No doubt I was still basically an autocratic paternalist (none of us could have been anything else in those days) but I was, unconsciously and very slowly, preparing for change as change became more practical and necessary. I was helped in this by the noticeable appreciation of the Africans, which I suppose pleased my vanity, and the growing disfavour of a considerable proportion of the white population—'He even invites Kaffirs to his house!'—which stimulated my natural bloodymindedness. In fact, I invited very few Africans to my house. It would have been senseless to invite the ordinary villager or labourer, with whom I could scarcely communicate, and if I had he would have looked at the plates and cups and things with trepidation and been very ill-at-ease. We should have both sat like fishes out of water, if fishes could sit. I occasionally asked one or two of the clerks, whom I knew well, to come to tea. I even had some hesitation about that, for they could hardly refuse if they did not want to come; and I had a horror of appearing to be like a duchess taking oranges to the poor. But they came, and were glad to come, not only for the novelty and the cakes and sandwiches that they could not afford but for the conversation and perhaps the small comfort that the colour bar was not entirely universal.

The colour bar, at this stage, did not worry the villager or migrant labourer very much, but it did distress the more evoluée Africans. It was an insidious thing. Social bars exist all over the world however much people may pretend otherwise, and the educated Africans had their own social bar. Colour added a very nasty quality to the social barrier which would have inevitably existed between the races. It was contagious: a little of it rubbed off on to all of us and a thick coating covered many. It was experienced at its most vicious extreme by one of my clerks.

His proud parents came in from their village to see him, and to stay with him for a week or two, having walked for many miles to the railway and spent nearly twenty-four hours in a slow train. At the end of their stay he asked for an hour off to see them on to the train. He wore his best white duck suit and his new shoes for the occasion. He came back to my office crying, not with filial affection, but with humiliation and rage. His suit and shoes were filthy. A white railway steward, after screaming abuse at him had emptied a bucket of slops over him as the train pulled out and laughed at the results, leaning out of the window as the train disappeared.

I said I would report this to the police, ask them to try to trace the man so that he could be charged with assault. The clerk did not want this. He doubted if he could recognize the man. He added that he was black and the man was white. I knew what he meant, although in this instance his suppositions would have been proved wrong by the police and the courts.

I sent him home for the day, to recover. It took longer than that. Some fifteen years later when he was visiting Lusaka from Nyasaland where he was then working, he came to see me to say Hallo and have a chat.

'I suppose you are what we call a political agitator now' I said cheerfully.

'What made you think that?' he asked.

I did not tell him.

Then he added, grinning, 'As a matter of fact I do lead a branch of the African National Congress.'

There were, of course, Europeans in all walks of life who treated Africans with consideration, but many did not. The whites were a very mixed lot, Britons, South Africans, Rhodesians, and, particularly in the copper mining towns, Cypriots, Greeks, Americans and other foreigners. Few of them took any real interest in the Protectorate or its people and there were very few genuine settlers except amongst the farmers.

White women were often as bad as men in their hatred of Africans and in their conduct towards them. Some women shop assistants were among the worst of the screeching abusers; and for a man to be abused by a woman in public—she could give him hell in private—was particularly shameful in African eyes. The educated Africans in white collar jobs were treated even more contemptuously by the worst elements in the white population than were the rest of the black population, and, of course, they felt the humiliation more.

The Africans had many shortcomings which they could not help but which could be extremely irritating to a European practising Western skills and living a Western life. The primitive villager who had come to work in the town, to return home with a little money after two or three years, was still a villager. He had little understanding of whatever work he was doing and no feeling for the strange tools he was using, which he often ruined as a result. The white man's temper, more easily frayed in the tropics than in his home country, was often vented on his workers. The Africans did not mind that greatly. It was what came from the white man's heart that hurt and that they judged him by.

I once got very angry with my cook and abused him badly. When my temper recovered I went into the kitchen and said I was sorry, which according to general white opinion, I should never have done ('They only take it as a sign of weakness').

He smiled and said, 'It's all right, bwana. We know by your eyes that you are not one of those that hate black people.'

CHAPTER ELEVEN

'Mutende'

'YOU VISIT LUSAKA once a week to hold court,' said my old enemy, the Secretary for Native Affairs. 'Could you possibly take on the editorship of *Mutende* there? You can, of course, refuse. The Chief Justice is furious that you should even be asked, but then you are only seconded to him . . . half of you. Your future still lies with the Administration.'

The suspicion of a sting in the tail of his remarks did not worry me, but I liked the idea of editing a paper, so I agreed to his proposal.

Mutende was a Government newspaper for Africans, issued fortnightly in the three major African languages and English, all printed side by side in the columns, rather like a schoolboy's Latin crib. Even to the illiterates, who used it for rolling cigarettes, it was good value for a penny. Unfortunately it was censored, and I often ran into trouble.

In 1938, I wrote a vicious attack on Hitler, which the Governor said would probably get him the sack as it ran counter to HMG's diplomacy at the time and a copy of the paper always went to the Colonial Office. That seemed to me to be irrelevant unless Hitler also received a copy, and he was not on my distribution list.

The Chief Justice also began to bother me more than usual. He was annoyed that I had gone against his wishes in taking on yet another job and he started sending me niggling comments on my cases. It was a relief to get away from legal work sometimes and tour the tribal areas for a week or two as an administrator, to see how the chiefs were carrying out the system of Indirect Rule, the latest brainchild of the Colonial Office.

It was not new, this idea of ruling the natives through their chiefs, the Colonial Office informed us. It had been the conception of that fine colonial administrator, Lord Lugard, and in Nigeria it had succeeded wonderfully in giving the natives a measure of local government by letting the chiefs and their councillors rule their areas under the supervision of the colonial administrators. This was not quite true. Lord Lugard was indeed a fine colonial administrator. In 1909 he had been faced with the impossible task of governing the vast Protectorate of Northern Nigeria with a handful of staff. He had done what several chartered companies in other parts of the Empire had done so economically before they handed over to the Colonial Office: he roped in the local native potentates to help him. They were protected, paid and left alone as long as they did what they were told. But the princes of the east and the Muslim emirs of Northern Nigeria were very different from the pagan and illiterate chiefs of Central Africa. Apart from Barotseland, which was and always had been a separate native state in Northern Rhodesia, ruled through an intelligent and educated paramount, there were only three or four paramount chiefs (the only two I ever had dealings with were usually drunk) and the rest were minor chiefs. Some were good rulers, some were not, and some were not hereditary chiefs at all but men appointed by early administrators and as such not highly regarded by their tribes.

I had seen a little evidence of the rule of past paramount chiefs—several men with a hand chopped off for an offence against the chief, a xylophone player in the chief's band, blinded because he had tried to run away, and so on. These practices had long since been stopped, but they reflected the customs of the ruling society in which many of the chiefs, who were mostly old men, were brought up. That background, it seemed to me, was too close for them to be successful administrators in the way that we wanted them to administrate.

The new Chief Secretary, who had come to us from the Bahamas, visited me to look round the Boma.

'Where' he asked challengingly 'do you keep your chiefs' cheque books and bank statements?'

'Nowhere' I replied. 'They have none.'

'Why not?' he asked. 'You have presumably organized Native Treasuries by now. You have had plenty of time.'

I said the chiefs could not write. I supposed they could put a thumb print on cheques filled in by me and which, like bank statements, they could not read. But as I had to keep detailed records of their revenue and expenditure anyway it seemed easier to give them a small imprest from the Boma safe.

'We have' I added encouragingly 'made a *start* on Native Treasuries. They are issuing marriage licences and bicycle licences and so on.'

'But each Treasury must have a clerk. Why can't the clerk sign cheques and run the accounts?'

'Because I am allowed two pounds a month for his pay and no clerk who can do more than write a name on a licence will take the job.'

It was the Chief Secretary's visit that inspired me to go off on tour and see how the chiefs were making out. The senior chief of the district was doing a brisk business in marriage licences, which the people wanted—they had no intention of paying bicycle or any other licences—and the cash collected tallied nicely with the counterfoils of the licences. Some bright villager had observed that the price of the licence was printed on it. It was sixpence, but the chief had been charging a shilling. A small crowd had gathered at his village by the time I arrived.

'The chief says the price has gone up. Has it?' they asked. I told them that it had not, and took the chief back with me to the Boma, where he received a short sentence from the district court for embezzlement.

The Indirect Rule system was later expanded to include judicial duties, Chiefs Courts, and other activities. It made more work than it saved and it never worked well except eventually in a few areas which had progressive chiefs and councillors. The clerks were shockingly badly paid and even the chief's 'subsidy' (pay) was a miserable pittance. There was a good deal of corruption which meant that we had to review all cases and hear many appeals.

Given more time, better education for the chief's heirs, more and better staff for them and more supervisory staff to guide them, the system could have led to reasonable local government in the rural areas if life had stood still in them.

When African National politics reared its head, the Government tried, and failed, to use the chiefs in an attempt to divide and rule, but the chiefs were black and the nationalists were black and even though the chiefs may not have liked the politicians much, their common colour forged a bond between them.

The Flag-Wagger

There was no African Nationalism yet, but now came the Second World War. It was the War which was to prepare the ground in which these first seeds of nationalistic feeling ripened into African Nationalism and the African National Congress.

CHAPTER TWELVE

The War

'THE WORD IS PURPLE' said a muffled, conspiratorial voice from Lusaka. I put the 'phone down, opened the Secret safe and studied the appropriate file. Its contents included 'The Plan for the Defence of Broken Hill', compiled by the Provincial Commissioner and approved by the War Office in London. One part of the plan concerned defence against enemy air raids.

Farmer Roy, on the outskirts of the town, had a large herd of cattle: he was the only farmer who had. Upon warning of an approaching air raid, which surely would be at night, Roy's cattle were to be rounded up and driven miles away into the bush, where hurricane lamps were to be lit and attached to their horns. The lights of the town would be extinguished and the enemy aircraft be deceived into dropping their bombs on Roy's cows.

At the first quick reading it seemed a splendid idea, apart from the difficulty of selling it to Roy and the fact that there was nothing for hundreds of miles in any direction to warn us of approaching aircraft. Somebody might ring up, I supposed. When I began to consider the likely behaviour of Roy's cattle and the fragility of hurricane lamps I discarded the plan. In fact, no bombers could have reached us from any enemy base without landing to refuel on British or Allied territory, where they would have had a great deal of trouble with Customs and Immigration and the local Defence Force. Our own, all white, Volunteer Defence Force was certainly ready for anything. I was one of its enthusiastic privates.

My immediate duty under the Plan was to inform the public of Broken Hill that we were at war, which they had already heard earlier from the BBC. The next instruction was to call out the local detachment of the Defence Force, so I ordered the Major to mobilize all his troops, less one (I had too many things to do). They mobilized outside my office. 'Where,' they asked enthusiastically, 'are we going?'

I said I had no idea but that they were supposed to be packed up and carrying some rations and it did not look as though they were.

'Rations?' they said, and hurried off home for supplies.

Some hours later, another colour was murmured into my ear. 'You can demobilize now,' I said to the Major.

'Why?' he asked, somewhat peeved. 'We're at war, dammit.'

I said I did not know.

The Regiment—African troops, white officers—arrived by rail, was accommodated for the night and departed by road to Somaliland where it subsequently fought its first action against the Italians and suffered considerable losses.

My Cadet had been called up, my Clerk of Court and my Secretary had gone sick, and cases were piling up in my courts down the line. So, having dealt with the Plan, I left the Boma to my African clerks and departed on circuit.

It was at Mazabuka, during the lunch adjournment, that a man in the bar asked me if I had heard the news. He handed me a copy of the *Livingstone Mail*, our only newspaper, a weekly, which had come out the day before and taken another day to reach Mazabuka. There was a total strike of Africans on the Copperbelt; there had been serious clashes with the police and bigger trouble was expected. The Broken Hill Defence Force Detachment had been mobilized and was on its way to the mines.

Copper was our major contribution to the war, and it seemed to me to be more important than the few cases left on the list, so I adjourned the Court and caught a goods train to Broken Hill, where a man at the Drill Hall gave me a uniform and various pieces of equipment. I caught the Mail Train north and changed in a compartment but could not get my ammunition pouches on right. I tried them upside down, sideways and all ways without success. There was clearly some cunning way of fitting them that I had not learned. It would be humiliating to report my presence to the Major when I reached Kitwe and ask him to fix my pouches for me. So I went to the Kitwe Police Station first, with the pouches dangling in my hand, and asked the Police Commandant if he could put them on for me.

He looked at the pouches and said 'They've given you two left-hand ones. I'll give you a right-hand one of ours; you'll be all right then.'

The War

Our Detachment would have quickly restored peace on the mines had it not already restored itself. At night we rode around in lorries with our bayonets fixed in order to impress the strikers, but they always seemed to be in bed.

I was glad when the Governor, as Commander-in-Chief of the Forces sent a telegram to the Major ordering my return to civil duties. There was nothing exciting happening and the food was terrible.

Guarding things at night that nobody had the slightest intention of attacking was in vogue at Broken Hill when I got back and the Defence Force was becoming depressing, when we were suddenly mobilized again. Italy had joined the war and everybody knew we were going to fight the Italians in East Africa and they weren't much good, all of which was cheering.

It turned out to be embarrassing. Having told my baffled domestic staff that I was off to fight the Italians, I joined the gang in the Drill Hall for a few hours. The Provincial Commissioner, back from leave, was now doing the mobilizing, but the form was the same. Shortly before midnight he demobilized us, and did not know why. In the morning, when I was awakened by the houseboy, who seemed quite unsurprised, I said I was not going to fight the Italians after all. 'Yes, Bwana' was all he said.

I went to Lusaka instead, transferred once more, as an Assistant Secretary for Native Affairs in the holy Secretariat.

The Native Affairs Division of the Secretariat was much more efficient and better informed that I had thought. The work was all paper work, which is possibly why I can remember very little of it. I was in it for less than a year anyway. It did its best to protect native interests; it provided answers to astonishing Parliamentary questions from Westminster and from the local Legislature; it supplied the Colonial Office with masses of detailed information, including the total number of village goats in the Protectorate; it drew up ancestral charts when any dispute concerning the rightful successor to a chieftainship arose. But it lacked humour and the human touch and it was not exciting. Nor was the Defence Force, though it did sometimes provide some comic relief.

We were occasionally engaged in serious military exercises such as the attack on Lusaka Airport. The Airport had been taken by the enemy, who were dug in at the far end of the runway and possessed a few rifles and blank cartridges.

We marched in a column of threes to our end of the runway. The Major then left us and went into the Airport buildings where there was a bar—it was a hot and thirsty day. We were left with a Lieutenant and a Corporal.

At the edge of the runway the Lieutenant shouted, 'You are about to be bombed by enemy aircraft. Open order!'

We opened order, and the Lieutenant walked off to the Airport buildings too. We wandered on until the Corporal yelled, 'You are now under shell fire—Arrow Head formation!' We arrow-headed.

The Lieutenant, a farmer who had actually been a Lieutenant in the previous war, reappeared, and enquired what we thought we were doing. We told him we were arrow-heading.

'What the hell for?' he asked.

We assured him that it was at the Corporal's wish. Left to our own devices we would have remained in open order.

He rebuked the Corporal. It appeared that we were not being shelled. We should have been in extended order.

We extended, and the enemy opened fire. The Major reappeared. The firing seemed to have put him in a bad temper.

'What in God's name do you think you're doing?' he enquired.

We told him that we were in a sort of extended line, as directed by the Lieutenant.

He said, 'You bloody fools, you're under fire! You should be scattered in the cover of the bush each side of the runway, outflanking the enemy, stealing up on them.'

We looked at the Lieutenant. He stood up for us. There was an argument. The Lieutenant lost it and followed the mollified Major back to the bar. Right and left we entered the bush, sat down and advised the Corporal to attack. He consented and we rushed the enemy from all sides. They joined us under the shade of various trees.

It was now dusk and the Corporal, after a consultation in the Airport buildings, said we were to await orders for night manoeuvres. As night fell, it became very chilly. The trickle of deserters became a flow. I suppose the Corporal reported to the bar, but the Major never mentioned the matter to us.

It was all a waste of time. I had a lot of work to do and my attendance of parades became erratic until I was prosecuted for not attending one.

The Chief Secretary to the Government had a working arrangement with the Defence Force Commander to give leave to a civil servant not to attend a parade if he had urgent work to do at the time. I qualified for the leave, but the Defence Force Commander, without telling anybody, had just ended the arrangement, which he had always disliked.

The Lusaka Detachment Commander phoned me to say that I must appear at the Court, so recently my Court, in uniform. I regretted that I could not because it was against the law; I was not allowed to wear uniform except on military duty and this was a Civil Court. When the day of the trial came the prosecutor and witnesses all appeared in uniform and the Resident Magistrate made some very nasty remarks on my civilian garb. I referred him to the relevant section of the Defence Force Ordinance, which seemed to dismay him somewhat.

At the end of the evidence, I said I had no case to answer. The Resident Magistrate said there was abundant *prima facie* evidence. I agreed that had I been a member of the Defence Force this would have been so but I had only signed on for six months, as many people had at the start, hoping to get to the war before the end of that period, and wishing to be free to get to it if by that time I had not. The six-months period had ended several months previously.

The Resident Magistrate said the period had been extended to the duration of the war. When I explained that the Regulation covered only recruits joining the Force after the date of the Regulation, he said 'You're right. Case dismissed, and I should like to make the observation that ex-Private Franklin has been attending parades for the last few months out of the goodness of his heart.' Subsequently I received an unsolicited discharge certificate from the C.O. of the Defence Force. It read

'*Character:* Good.
Qualities as a soldier: Nil.'

I thought that was fair enough.

The results of the case were unexpected. I was quite popular with a good many miners and others who had been similarly prosecuted and fined £5. They all asked for their fivers back. I was not so popular with Colonel the Honourable Stewart Gore-Browne.

He and Welensky, later Sir Roy Welensky, Prime Minister of the ill-fated Federation of Rhodesia and Nyasaland, were the leaders of the unofficial members of the Legislative Council. Until now I had been only dimly aware of the existence of this Council, which had developed—and was now developing fast—from the old Advisory Council in Livingstone, a body which had included the local chemist, a farmer and one or two other unofficials as well as the heads of several key government departments. It had been of little importance, for the Governor had run the show.

Ultimately he still ran it, with his 'reserved powers' in the background if needed, through his Executive Council of officials (Cabinet); but holding the fort in the Legislative Council where white unofficials could just manage, if they all stuck together, to outvote the officials, was tricky. It soon became very difficult, as Westminster increased the number and power of the white unofficial members of the Legislature, putting several of them in the Executive Council.

The unofficial members were now a force to be reckoned with. There was no love lost between most of the staff of the Colonial Service and the politicians, but in the ivory towers of my outstations I neither liked nor disliked them. I heard very little of them, and even when I had a brush with Roy Welensky and another with Colonel Gore-Browne I was unaware that politicians in general were of any real importance. It was in Lusaka that I discovered that they were. There I was transferred from the Secretariat to yet another different job: that of running the Government Information Service.

This move meant more pay and escape from the Secretariat, and I welcomed the change. Colonel Gore-Browne did not. He saw the Governor and said that I was not the right man for the job. The Governor disagreed with him and reminded the Colonel that politicians had nothing to do with Service appointments.

Running the new Government Information Service took me to various parts of the Empire closer to, or actually embroiled in, the war. The work was partly concerned with war propaganda and it was easy enough to extend that to embrace Troops' Welfare. We had six battalions of African troops serving abroad and nothing was being done by the civilian population for their welfare.

Having set up a Troops Welfare organization and a Home News Service for the battalions and done a few other things that East Africa Command approved of, I was visited by a General from Nairobi who was staying at Government House in Lusaka for a few days.

The Governor had said that he would release me for active service if I could produce evidence that I would be of more value to the Army than to the Colonial Service, adding that he did not think that likely. I wondered if he had been sent a copy of my Defence Force discharge certificate. Perhaps I could impress this General and he could provide the evidence. I explained the situation to him.

He said, kindly, that I would be wasted as a soldier. As a last resort, I suggested that East Africa Command must need an official war correspondent to serve its Information Unit in Nairobi, which published a magazine, and to supply the local papers of the territories with news of their battalions. If he would kindly tell the Governor . . .

He did. The Governor said that, provided I did not neglect any civil duties in Lusaka, whenever our own troops were in action I could go and write about it. In the event this was not as exciting as it might have been, owing to the disinclination of the generals in the field to give me advance notice of their battle plans and I arrived everywhere too late to get into action, except once. I now visited Nairobi fairly often and used to wander around the city, observing. The slums of the African quarter were even more appalling than the worst of ours but the attitude of the Nairobi whites to the blacks seemed to be not quite so bad as it was in Northern Rhodesia. Even so, the inevitable poverty of the Africans was the same in Nairobi as in Broken Hill.

Madagascar was my first overseas expedition. The shooting was long over by the time I got there and three of our battalions had been sent there only as garrison troops.

As I stepped off the troopship at Diego Suarez, one of the filthiest seaport towns in the world, I was met by an officer who said, 'It is my duty to tell you that there are three hundred and ninety whores in Diego. One of them is believed to be free of venereal disease at present. We warn all newcomers.' I found that easy to believe as we drove through the squalor and poverty of the town until we reached the French residential quarter. Even that was far below British colonial standards.

The town was undamaged—there had been very little fighting and that mostly round the fort up the hill—but it had been blockaded for some time, which had presumably increased its general air of misery. Its climate was foul and the sticky heat unbearable. Dengue fever, dysentery and other tropical diseases flourished. The island was said to be the worst of the French colonies, and a punishment station to which the worst of its military and civil officers were sent.

The whole of Diego Suarez stank of rum. The smell was particularly strong whenever a car passed by. The French had no petrol but plenty of rum, so they used it instead. It was a local product and not very good but it was the only drink on the island and therefore acceptable if you could get your lips to the glass before it was smothered with flies. The rum was the only remotely cheering thing I found in Madagascar, and I left the island wondering why on earth the French wanted it.

Towards the end of the war with Japan, the troops of East Africa Command were in action in Burma, clearing out the enemy from the Kabaw valley. They had cleared it by the time I arrived to report on the operation. Thankfully, there were still little pockets of resistance elsewhere, behind the Sittang-Moulmein line, which was held by British and Indian troops. Eventually I found one, but it took a long time. To get there a Catalina (a long range flying boat used then for anti-submarine patrols) flew me across the Indian Ocean from Mombasa, via Mahe in the Seychelles and a coral ring called Diego Garcia.

The Seychelles are incredibly beautiful, but hot and sticky at sea level. In those islands, so an old timer told me, fish are three for a penny and women are three for a fish, but I do not think that that was why the Chief Secretary of Northern Rhodesia accepted appointment as Governor of the islands. Nevertheless, there he was, alone in a rambling Government House made of wood with a tin roof and a magnificent dining table surrounded by chairs bearing the Royal crest.

At dinner on the evening of my arrival the Governor sat at one end of it, surveying an empty expanse of polished mahogany and put me on his right, so that we would not need to shout at each other from opposite ends. Our two places were laid with splendid silver and cut glass. A servant brought in a small tin of steak and kidney pudding—I think it must have been intended for one person—and skilfully extracted it onto a serving dish without breaking the crust.

'If it were not for the rations of the R.A.F. Catalina dropping in occasionally,' observed the Governor sadly, 'it would be fish again. There used to be a ship about once a month, but not now.'

He was pleased to see me; I reminded him of old times. He told me about the islands. There was a small fishing industry with, at present, no market; much copra with no ships to carry it; and for the rest, the island abounded in spices and tropical fruits and almost everything that he did not wish to eat. The people, he said, were idle but happy. I found that easy to believe. There was no colour bar: everybody was coloured. Pirates of all nations, and later the French colonists with the slaves they brought with them from Africa, had interbred for centuries, unconsciously producing the only solution to the colour problem.

The Seychelles were, and still are, one of the many small island colonies which never wanted, and still do not want, independence. Several such colonies have had independence thrust upon them and in due course this will probably be the fate of the remainder. They must be such a nuisance to the Foreign Office, which now deals with the vestiges of Colonial and Commonwealth affairs.

That the Catalina found Diego Garcia seemed to me a miracle. I spent most of my time sitting in the perspex blister with the guns near the tail, looking down at the sea, blue-gleaming and white-speckled, and up at the pale, empty sky. We flew from early morning until mid-afternoon, out of radio contact and with no sight of ship or land, by the compass, the sun and the yellow patches in the sea made, at intervals, by dropping cylinders of chemicals through a calibrated cylinder which registered our drift.

Diego Garcia, a coral circle round a lagoon, backed by a strip of coconut palms, had a population of one half-caste with a large family—living, one imagined, on coconuts—and about half-a-dozen RAF personnel covered with heat rash.

The next stop was a seaplane base in Ceylon, north of Colombo, where the fat servant who brought me tea in the morning solemnly informed me he was starving. Outside the wooden bungalow the place was festooned, as the whole of Ceylon seemed to be, with bread fruit, bananas, mangoes, coconuts, and countless other fruits. I presumed that the servant had no taste for fruit, took the hint and doubled the tip.

The driver of the army truck that drove me to the airport to catch the plane for Calcutta was contemptuous of the villagers and their lack of road sense, which was, admittedly, noticeable. He was not one of the army's most careful drivers, and missed by a hair's breadth one man who fell over on the road. 'Bloodie coolie,' he said, driving on, 'he's not hurt.' It seemed he was right, but the coolie was clearly not pleased. Looking back, I could see him, now standing up and shaking his fist. The British Image had not been improved.

During the drive into Calcutta from the airport my ideas of India as a country of romance and glamour began to change. It was night when we entered the city, and we passed a large and brilliant electric light over a chemists shop. It read 'VENUS AND DIAMOND. SPECIALISTS IN LOVE PHILTRES AND VENEREAL DISEASES'.

In the city I took off my shirt and wrung the sweat out of it in a flow. The heat struck like a physical blow every time one had to leave the swirl of punkahs in a room and go out. It was only after taking a cold bath and not drying, letting the punkahs evaporate the water, that I could sleep. Thank God I served the Empire in Africa!

Calcutta was filthy and grossly overpopulated. There was a cholera epidemic on. The untouchables slept on the pavements and in the railway station, where they were so thick on the ground that one had to pick one's way carefully to avoid treading on them. Their physical condition was appalling. They had their own people to blame for that; the high caste Indians and the wealthy ones—the ones that were talking about home rule for India and, I thought, would not get it. The British Raj would surely never give way to wealthy, love-philtre-selling oppressors of the poor.

At the burning ghat on the outskirts of the city by the river, I watched the burning of the dead, each body on a separate pyre of timber and surrounded by mourning relatives who had somehow scraped together enough rupees for a funeral, weeping and wailing bitterly. Among them wandered 'holy men' with braided hair styles and paint and necklaces of pieces of animal bones and bracelets of teeth. Amazing. They sold charms and incantations to the mourners. I should have known that the curse of witchcraft was not confined to Africa.

Not without some difficulty, I eventually arrived in Rangoon, having travelled by plane, water-boat (a boat for carrying water) and paddle steamer. Soon after my arrival at the Press Camp, I learned that many Burmese had been on the side of the enemy until it became obvious that the Japanese were going to lose. Some of these Burmese Nationalists had even fought in Japanese uniforms, but more often they had just given general assistance to the enemy, spied for them and done a little guerrilla skirmishing. I also discovered that Burma was to be given its independence when the war ended.

A wealthy Burmese invited the correspondents at the Press Camp to a cocktail party one evening. His house was magnificent and beautifully appointed with oriental art treasures worth a fortune. Against one wall of the lounge there was a huge screen, elaborately carved in Burmese teak, the centre piece of which was the rising sun.

Our host introduced us to his friends. I remember that one was a professor at Rangoon University, another a consultant doctor and a third a lawyer.

The American correspondent with us greatly admired the house and slyly commented on how lucky our host had been not to have had his house commandeered by Japanese officers, who, if they did not loot their quarters completely, always left them in a filthy and dilapidated condition. Our host quickly assured us that, though his house had been commandeered, the carved screen had saved it from harm. 'The Japanese were sun-worshippers' he reminded us. 'They prayed in front of the screen and treated the house with great respect.' He soon got on to the subject of independence.

'We shall soon be governing Burma' he said. 'The British Government has promised us that.' He made it clear that it was the elite of Burma including himself that would govern, not the ignorant masses, who would however rejoice in their freedom from the British imperial yoke.

I doubted this, rather bluntly, and added, 'It seems to me that here, as in India, you treat your poor, your coolies and rickshaw men, like dogs—far worse than any British imperialist does.'

'Not like dogs' he replied, 'but like the inferior people that they are. They understand that. They don't mind.'

'If you think that, then you are not fit to govern Burma' I responded.

I firmly believed that British rule was the best thing that had ever happened to Burma or any other of our colonial possessions. I still believe that, in its day, it was certainly better than the rule, or misrule, that it replaced. I had by now heard in India similar talk about self-rule. From what I had seen there too, it seemed impossible that Britain would hand over the people to men of the sort who expected to govern Burma.

I drove a Jeep around parts of Burma, looking for African troops in action, through improbable places like Gyobinyauk, until at last I found an African battalion lodged in a Buddhist monastery. The monks, who were said to be always on the Japanese side, had fled. The battalion had one company in a more advanced post near the edge of the mountains and from there I was permitted to set off, with film camera and sten gun, with a fighting patrol which was to attack and destroy a Japanese camp in the mountains. A Japanese foraging patrol from this camp had recently been engaged by one of our patrols.

Except for the abundance of weapons, it was rather like setting out from the Boma on a tour of the villages. Many of the soldiers at the end of the column were carrying four-gallon tins of rations on their heads. We camped for the first night at a Burmese village over which the war had trampled. Early in the morning I was given a tin of black boot polish and requested to smear it over my face and arms. It would not be a good thing to be recognized by the enemy as a white officer.

During the morning we passed the scene of the recent patrol action in the teak-forested mountains. There were bullet marks in the trees all over the place, but I was told that nobody had been hit. That night I found myself lying on a little sloping bamboo platform with a large hole in the ground in front of it into which I was supposed to slide, protectively, should the need arise. Sentries were posted. Silence, no lights, no smoking, were commanded. I lay on the platform, terrified, looking into the forest and seeing a

Japanese soldier behind every tree, until a snake fell on me from the palm leaved roof over the platform. I froze until it crawled away. After that I forgot the Japanese but remained terrified of snakes until dawn, when we were to go into action.

It was a splendid action; a model example of how war should be fought. On a path through the forest we met a file of armed Keren tribesmen. They were laden with sacks of rice and festooned with items of Japanese equipment. Through our Burmese interpreter we asked them what they had been doing.

'Looting the Japanese camp during the night,' they said happily.

'Very brave chaps,' we said, 'creeping past their sentries in the darkness and pinching their rice before they woke up.'

'Oh no,' they said. 'The Japanese ran away yesterday evening. They knew you were coming . . . and so did we.'

Further on, from the slope of a hill we looked down on the camp, a surprisingly big one.

'Might be somebody left' said the Major cunningly.

I got some excellent cine shots as the troops charged the camp. The noise of the firing was exhilarating. The phosphorus grenades made a splendid show. There was no return fire.

Disconsolate, but relieved, I returned to the monastery.

There was a rival to the Buddhist monastery, about ten miles from it: the Catholic church in the mountains above the plain where the Burmese grew their rice and fed the Buddhist priests. The mountains were Keren country and many of the Kerens were Catholic converts. I met the priest of this church in a Keren village on my way back to base and learned a little about the tribe. Before this, I had not even known that there were any tribes in Burma before this, nor that there were many different tribes in India and, accordingly, different languages.

The priest had not joined in the evacuation before the Japanese occupation. He had stayed with his parishioners and led a fugitive life with them until the Japanese left.

'I knew the British would come back,' he said, 'but as time went on the Kerens became disheartened. They wouldn't believe me. But I found a tin of bully beef on the edge of the forest one day. It looked quite new, probably left behind from an RAF airdrop to a guerilla unit. The Kerens knew what it was all right. They used to buy it in the village store. There's your proof, I told them. The

British are coming back. They accepted that. They were delighted.'

I said I was glad that *somebody* in Burma liked British rule.

'When the Burmese take over the government,' he said, 'the Kerens will fight them; so will the Shans and the other tribes. They hate the Burmese.' And the tribes did fight. They still do when they get a chance.

On the flight back to Lusaka via London I had plenty of time to think. Wherever I had been with our African troops I had noticed that they were no longer the simple villagers that they had been. Off-duty they questioned, they complained.

They were loyal, with a curious kind of personal loyalty to the great King in England, whom they thought must be an incredibly powerful chief. This I had heard before from many African villagers. But they had volunteered (no Africans were conscripted) by no means entirely from patriotic motives, but for adventure and excitement and particularly for the pay and uniforms, and rations which were much better than they could get at home.

They did not talk politics to me and I doubt if they thought politics at that time, but it did occur to me that when they got back home they would not be content with the life they had led there before. They had listened and watched. They had seen new worlds. They had new ideas, and one of them was about their own worth; they had fought side-by-side with the white men.

My own ideas were changing too. The problems of bringing the backward peoples of the colonies carefully up to western civilization and standards of living over a necessarily long period of time were far greater than I had thought. In the countries of East and Central Africa and in India, Ceylon and Burma, which I had now seen, the problems were as bad as in Northern Rhodesia. In India and Ceylon they were in fact worse, owing to the density of the population. Our Africans were sometimes hungry after a bad season's crops and in general suffered from malnutrition, but throughout India men died like flies from sheer starvation during their periodic famines, and in the cities they died regardless of famines.

In all these countries there were the conflicts of tribalism and many different religions. We had Mohammedanism in Northern Rhodesia quite apart from the competing Christian churches (which so baffled the people) but we had nothing like the bitter differences of religion in the East and nothing like the untouchables.

Witchcraft, ignorance and disease were common denominators. The Indian traders who controlled most of the retail trade in all these countries (except for the Chinese in Burma) cared little who governed them so long as they were allowed to cheat the ignorant poor, something they constantly did. The tribesmen, both in Africa and the East, liked us and were happy with British rule. The rich, educated upper class despised the masses and hated the British. We had no such class yet in East and Central Africa and I hoped that when we had they would treat their own people well, but I had an uneasy feeling that a pattern was beginning to develop of the way the Empire was going. And everywhere there was the colour bar and the arrogance of the white settler.

I broke my journey back to Africa with a few weeks in London. In the little shops of the suburbs, the women shop assistants addressed me as 'Love'. I got lost driving through a slum and stopped outside a very sleazy looking pub and asked two very tough looking types if they could direct me, expecting a surly answer. They were very pleasant indeed and took a lot of trouble to make sure I could follow their directions.

I was in Piccadilly on 'V.J.' night after the Japanese had surrendered. The place was packed solidly with solid and happy Britons. They were one people, one nation, and I loved them and was proud to be one of them. But how long had it taken to build this nation? And how long would it take Northern Rhodesia and the rest of the Empire countries to build theirs?

CHAPTER THIRTEEN

Very Odd Jobs

NONE of the real privations of the war were felt in Northern Rhodesia, but it did have the effect of holding back the rapid development of the country, and particularly of the social services which the African population so badly needed. For the past few years the graph of development had been rising steeply in step with the development of the copper mines and the increasing revenues from them. It continued to rise, and it would have shot up, as it did after the war, but for the lack of skilled manpower and of imported materials, and the price control on copper which Britain necessarily fixed at the beginning of the war. It particularly affected my new department which needed skills and equipment that did not exist in the Protectorate and could not be obtained from outside it until the war ended.

The Government, prompted like all colonial governments by the Colonial Office, started the Information Service primarily to boost the Protectorate's war effort. It had started with a weekly newsletter, a small transmitter for broadcasting, and a distribution service for the British Ministry of Information propaganda material sent out from London. None of this, except part of the broadcasting, was of much use to Africans. The Administrative Officer who had been running it left on transfer and promotion as Colonial Secretary to the chilly and windswept Falkland Islands, populated by some two thousand Scotsmen and innumerable sheep. He must have found it quite a change from Africa.

In 1942, I was required to build the Office up into a Department using all the modern media of publicity, films, photographs, posters *etcetera*. The objective was not only to directly encourage the war effort but to popularize the Government by informing the people about what it was doing and how and why it was doing it. Britain had its back to the wall and it was important to avoid any trouble in the colonies.

The Flag-Wagger

Having no qualifications whatever for this work enabled me to bring an open, if not blank, mind to it with an enthusiasm undeterred by ignorance. It was a position I had been in many times before.

It seemed to me that a diet of government propaganda alone would not be very satisfying. The people should be kept happy with some entertainment. The Africans at Broken Hill had enjoyed the cinema, while it lasted; that would be a good line to start with. Without films or projectors it would have to be a modest start but perhaps I could find a good amateur with a 16 mm camera and projector who could make films. 16 mm equipment would be small enough to put in the back of the car and take around for shows. With a staff of two Colonial Service wives and an office boy one would need volunteer actors, but we could begin with little documentaries, instructive films like 'How to Mend a Bicycle'. I could use a mechanic from the Public Works Department for that.

That film, and many others, were eventually made but for a long time I was in the unhappy position of having, for the first time, more government funds than I could spend on doing the things that needed doing. I had been given a free hand. The Governor had said, 'If you can't get what you want from the Secretariat come to me'. But neither he nor anybody else could find me men and materials. They were just not available while the war lasted.

All I could do, at first, was to brighten up the *European Newsletter*. Circulation improved, but there were occasional setbacks. The war needed rubber, and the importation of non-essential rubber products was accordingly banned by our Controller of Imports. Golfers were hard hit and so one of the women on my staff produced a recipe for the resuscitation of old golf balls which she had found in a book. I put the recipe in the *Newsletter*. 'Boil the balls in water for ten minutes. When cool enough to handle, roll the balls on a board and they will come back into shape with all the cuts healed.' I knew that golfers would be grateful and waited for the fan mail. It came, from several golf club secretaries, one of whom enclosed his angry letter in a small package containing the remains of four golf balls. Their covers had split in all directions and strings of rubber festooned the inside of the parcel. I called for the book containing the recipe. It was a collector's piece, published at the end of the nineteenth century when gutta-percha balls were used.

I was rather dejected by this error, but confidence was soon to be restored by another incident concerning rubber. As an administrator I had learned the importance of touring my district and getting amongst the people. In this new job it was equally desirable to get around the country, talking and listening to black men and white.

There were rumblings of strikes from the white copper miners up north. Their discontents were said to include the general shortage of supplies. I decided to tour the Copperbelt and get some first-hand information. At Kitwe the Women's Institute required me to attend them. They were angry. It was obviously going to be one of those nasty meetings, easier to handle with men than with women.

I listened to a tirade against the Government Controller of Imports, to which I replied firmly; but I was unwise enough to invite questions on any point that might need further explanation. No audience should ever be given this opportunity. The speaker should end with grateful thanks, look anxiously at his watch and hurry away.

'Why' shouted an aggressive lady, 'has the Controller stopped the import of French letters and babies' napkins—aren't they essentials?' I agreed at once about the napkins and promised to urge the Controller to allow the import of both items, since the need for the second would be reduced by the availability of the first. The meeting ended in mutual admiration. When I got back to Lusaka there was no need to urge the Controller. He agreed at once; the logic was irresistible.

It was expeditions such as these that kept me from forgetting the vast territory outside the line-of-rail towns. They also kept me mindful of what I considered should be the real task of a colonial Government Information Department—mass adult education, in the widest sense of the word 'education'. The African Education Department was now really growing and it looked as though there would be schooling for all the children in about twenty years' time—it proved to be an optimistic estimate—but something needed to be done for the present *adult* population, many of whom had received no formal education whatever.

The only media I could use for this purpose at this time were *Mutende* and the embryonic broadcasting service, which transmitted for only one hour every evening. Half of that time and all the two extra hours on Sunday was allocated to European broadcasting.

This seemed to me unfair but there was more sense in this division than I had realised, for only the Europeans possessed radios. No African could afford to buy one. Such African listeners as we had, and they must have been very few, were domestic servants, allowed by their masters to listen to our broadcasts in the four main native languages, and a few villagers here and there, gathered round by a benevolent missionary or administrator in the rural areas.

Another major obstacle that I was unaware of for a long time was that few people of any colour could hear us anyway because of the erratic range of the little short-wave transmitter. It had been built by a local Post Office engineer, and our broadcasts could sometimes be heard in Livingstone in the south or a mining town in the north, and never anywhere over a really wide area.

Unaware of such trivia, I was shown the transmitter by the corporal of signals who attended it during its little performances. I was introduced to the studio by my predecessor before he left for the Falklands and shown how to twiddle the three knobs and operate the gramophone turntable. He said he would read the News and then leave me to handle the music programme. 'All you have to do is to read out the title of the record and give its make and number'. The microphone terrified me and the knobs and switches were more confusing than I had expected, but after the first two records I felt better. The third was an HMV production.

I announced it as 'A His Majesty's Voice record called "Impromptu in a Flat", by Schubert.' I immediately realized the 'His Majesty's' error, but there seemed no reason why a composer could not do something impromptu in a flat.

The announcement was well received by friends in Lusaka listening on the ground wave. 'Time we had a touch of humour in the programme,' they said. 'Thought up on the spur of the moment, too. Pretty good.'

I soon got to know every detail in the studio. It was a small room in the airport building with an office table for the homemade console, turntable and solitary microphone, and an armchair for visitors by the fireplace which was sealed off with a square of plywood to muffle the cries of owls nesting in the chimney top.

There was a casement window which came in handy whenever I invited an African choir from the local missions to give a recital. The room was too small to hold them and they would have blasted the microphone off the table anyway, so they sang from a field a few yards back from the open window through which the hymns wafted at a reasonable volume.

There were many breakdowns which sometimes lasted for days. The studio was connected to the transmitter by half a mile of overhead cable and in the rainy season the violent tropical storms blew everything down. Other interruptions were less easily accountable for. Whenever they occurred I would phone the corporal, if the phone was working, and ask him what was wrong. He seldom knew, so I would drive off to the transmitter house—an old Post Office store—and we would confer.

'Better ask the Post Office to look at it tomorrow,' was the usual decision until I kicked the transmitter hard in a fury one night, and it immediately came on. After that it was always kicked when it stopped and only if it did not respond did we call for Post Office help.

The Corporal's successor was a railway telegraphist. He was a more resourceful man and he discovered that the faults were often due to mice getting into the transmitter and chewing the wax insulated wires.

'We must get a station cat' he suggested 'and leave the back of the transmitter open so that it can get in. We'll shut it before we switch on.'

The cat did a splendid job until the telegraphist forgot about shutting the transmitter before switching on. The cat shot screeching through the window and never came back.

Although I gradually extended the broadcasting hours, the Africans were not getting much benefit from broadcasting, but they were getting more interested in the African newspaper, *Mutende*, and started writing occasional letters to the Editor. Some of these reflected the dissatisfaction of the educated class (educated, that is, by African not European standards). 'Why is our pay so small and the European's so big?' 'Who is this man Welensky who argues against the Government and the Colonial Office bwanas?'

There were by now a few African Welfare Societies in the urban areas, from which, much later, sprang the African National Congress political party. Their petitions to the District Commissioner or the central Government were mostly confined to modest requests for more amenities of one kind or another, but they too sometimes revealed dissatisfaction with, and fear of, the growing power of white settler politics led by Roy Welensky.

These views could not be published in *Mutende*, which was, of course, a Government newspaper, run by Civil Servants. Politics were banned from it. They would have infuriated the white copper miners and the politicians had they been published. The policy of the Colonial Service Government was to keep copper production running smoothly and to keep the peace with the 'Opposition', which Roy Welensky and his white politicians were actively and increasingly becoming, though not quite on Westminster lines: there were no means whereby they could bring down the Government and take over the reins.

I found it difficult to keep the peace when Roy Welensky objected to items in *Mutende* or wanted more broadcasting time for Europeans or thought that my press handouts of Legislative Council affairs gave more space to the Government side than to his—they were the only source of information that did.

The European daily paper was the *Bulawayo Chronicle*, which came up from Southern Rhodesia, and there was a Sunday paper, also from Southern Rhodesia. They both boosted Roy Welensky and damned the Colonial Office and its Colonial Service government in Lusaka. Both papers were owned by the Argus Company in Johannesburg. The South African influence and attitude, not only from the monopolist press but from the whites who came North in ever increasing numbers and even from as far as Kenya and Tanganyika seeking better pay and conditions, did no good to race relations.

The *Bulawayo Chronicle* was most inaccurate in its reporting of Northern Rhodesian Government activities and very biased in its comment on them. This was not surprising as at this time it had no staff reporter stationed in the Protectorate and, except when a staff reporter came North on a short tour, relied on local correspondents, most of whom were Welensky supporters whose strong dislike of Colonial Office rule was only surpassed by the *Bulawayo Chronicle* editor's hatred of it.

At a political meeting before his election, Welensky was asked the question 'What is your policy?'

His reply was, 'I don't need a policy. I'm just pro-settler'. In fact, that was all the policy he needed and, unlike most politicians, he never departed from it. It would have been an excellent policy if the population ratio had been reversed: it was twenty thousand whites and two million blacks, one to a hundred.

Neither Roy Welensky nor the editor of the *Bulawayo Chronicle* seemed able to understand that the British Government could not possibly hand over a black Protectorate to a handful of whites. But the editor was a man of good journalistic principles. I went down to Bulawayo to try to persuade him to take a more balanced line on what Southern Rhodesians called 'The Black North' and discovered that one of the things that annoyed him was the haughty attitude and tight-lipped silence of senior officials towards his visiting reporters. 'As for Governors,' he commented, 'they think they are God.'

I did not tell him that I knew that some superior officers were much too superior. Nor did I tell him that the present Governor was not at all godlike. I suggested that if he came on a tour of the North he would find that he was wrong. He agreed to come.

Back in Lusaka I reported to the Governor and suggested that he should invite the editor to stay a weekend at Government House during his tour.

'Good idea' he said. 'We had better tell everybody that he's coming round and to look after him and give him any news material he wants.'

The editor enjoyed his tour. The news and views of his paper on the Black North were a little better balanced thereafter, but I nevertheless decided to start a Press Section in the Department. The politicians did not like the idea at all.

I now sometimes came under political fire in the Legislative Council from Roy Welensky or one of his colleagues, not always unreasonably. Four-letter words were not then acceptable in broadcasting and their use in Lusaka Radio was rightly condemned by the Opposition. I had been away in Johannesburg in search of studio equipment and returned to something of an uproar in the Legislature. A farmer had complained to his local elected Member that foul words were being used by African broadcasters. His two dear old aunts from South Africa were visiting him and he thought they would enjoy the novelty of listening to kaffirs broadcasting, so he switched on to Radio Lusaka. They could not understand the language of the programme until it came to English words like f— and c—. He and his aunts were distressed and disgusted.

I did not believe the story. I knew my African announcers and readers would never use such language. I knew the farmer and his dislike of all things black and one thing white: the Colonial Service. I doubted the existence of his aunts and knew that no four-letter words could ever distress *him*.

Unfortunately, I had forgotten about our African plays, produced and acted, but not written, by a group of askari in training with the new battalion being formed in Lusaka. The plays were not written because the askari could neither write nor read. They thought up a plot of sorts, gathered round the microphone and let native wit have its way. These impromptu plays were sometimes staged in the villages and usually guyed somebody. I should have known that they sometimes guyed a white man, perhaps a missionary or a District Commissioner, but as a District Commissioner I had not seen a play that did.

By now there were community receivers dotted about the country in African town compounds and welfare halls in any areas where reception from our little transmitter was possible. Listeners were still few, but the number was growing. It was therefore desirable that the studio output should grow too, and become much more entertaining. Plays appeared to be the answer, but since they were not scripted the only check I could have on them was to ask for advance notice of the plot.

The play which the farmer's aunts had found offensive introduced a white police officer who was questioning a witness, an African woman, about a murder. It had, I discovered later, been very well done and delighted the listeners. The woman's lies and evasions and the policeman's inadequate knowledge of her language led him into a furious string of the dirtiest words in English, which every African recruit soon picked up on the parade ground.

Welensky, I heard, enjoyed the debate. He had a good sense of humour. We might have liked each other if our objectives had not been so completely in conflict.

There were other problems besides political ones: amateur anthropologists suggested that it was a waste of time and money to publish photographs in *Mutende*. They claimed that Africans could not interpret photographs, and that they often looked at them upside down. European art in the form of posters, said others, was quite unintelligible to Africans, and someone else suggested that taking voice recordings might be regarded as witchcraft. Most of the suggestions of this kind were nonsensical, but there was always the possibility of unknowingly writing or broadcasting something that would offend native custom. I had no time to worry about that and thought that any offence would probably be put down to the white man's ignorance and be disregarded. However, I did try one experiment to check the witchcraft theory concerning recordings. I knew that Africans believed that the tiniest part of a man, if it came into the possession of somebody else who wished its owner no good and handed it to a witchdoctor, could be used to bewitch him. This was the reason why the villager, when he cut his nails, carefully kept the parings and burned or buried them.

I recorded messages from some visiting chiefs to broadcast to their people at home. They were entranced when I played back the disc for them to hear. I gathered up the black floss made by the cutting needle and took it outside, saying, 'We'll burn it, so that witchdoctor can't get hold of it'. The floss went up with a puff of flame and black smoke which fascinated them. 'Like gunpowder,' they said. 'But it would have been no use to a witchdoctor. White men's magic is only for white men; ours is only for black.'

It was all rather uphill work. Even the Secretary for Native Affairs said that Africans did not want broadcasting and would never bother to listen to it. The politicians took a different view, that the Africans would certainly listen, 'and get wrong ideas into their heads'.

I had some volunteer help in the studio from several colleagues, in news-gathering from a few District Commissioners. Some others refused to assist in any way, regarding the Information Department as a very brash organization—which at this stage it was—and wondering what the devil an administrator was doing, dabbling in publicity work, playing with his useless toys.

Mercifully, I had the Governor, Sir John Waddington, solidly behind me, and that was all I needed. *He* did not think he was God, but I thought he was something rather like that. He was a quiet and able administrator of great humanity. He knew where his duty lay, in the uplifting of the African people, and his inclination ran with his duty. He had to conceal his distaste for politicians and his dislike for the leaders of the white Trade Unions of the copper mines (who were quite unconcerned about the badly underpaid African mineworkers). He handled both with firmness. Occasionally he indulged in a rather schoolboyish glee, which they failed to discern: and once he employed a brass band to advantage. A total strike of white miners was threatened on one of the mines, the output of which was vital to Britain at war. The tub-thumping Trade Union leader at this mine was a good-hearted type in many ways, but rather vain and quite illogical, which made him difficult to reason with, as I, and later the Governor, discovered. He had formed a brass band of strong-winded white miners and was very proud of it. 'We'll have a garden party and bring him and his band down to Government House instead of using the Regimental Band,' the Governor said to me. I ventured to doubt whether that would help reason to prevail.

'We'll see,' said the Governor, chuckling.

It was a splendid garden party. The Governor, a music-lover, endured the band with amiable fortitude and praised it lavishly in a little speech thanking it for its appearance. The bandsmen were very pleased, the Trade Union leader was almost overcome with delight and led the band through the town from the railway station when it arrived back on the Copperbelt. He then declared the strike off.

The possibilities available to a real administrator when negotiating are almost without limit.

CHAPTER FOURTEEN

The Saucepan

AS A CHILD I had seen desperate poverty in the streets of Woolwich. I remember being upset at the sight of a small procession of unemployed, half-starved men, who were singing a sad song: 'We are but English working men, we only seek our bread.' I even remember the tune. I had seen the desperate drunkenness of the poor. Cheap rotgut spirits were a temporary relief from the misery of the slums in which they lived. As I grew up I had watched that poverty and drunkenness disappearing in the face of better education and better pay. On home leaves from Africa I had noticed that the disappearing process and the betterment process were accelerating faster and faster.

The poverty and drunkenness in Africa were much worse than I had seen in England. The remedies, I was sure, were the same, though the difficulties of applying them were far greater. But I could at least use the inadequate media now at my disposal to spread a little education of a kind and to provide some entertainment outside the beerhalls, and I now used them to those ends.

The results were not at first very impressive, but they grew less unimpressive as time went on. Several experiments failed almost completely, like the mass literacy campaign and the little travelling demonstration circus to teach villagers things like mosquito control. They were too ambitious for the means available and perhaps my attitude was wrong. I was a little too determined that Africans ought to be done good to—by me.

With memories of African reaction to Charlie Chaplin in mind I decided to start the film section of the department, and engaged 'Young Louis', a timekeeper on the mines and the only man I could find who knew anything at all about films. We scoured film libraries abroad for suitable films and Louis made his own films, outside in the street or in a village. We assembled a small fleet of mobile cinema vans and two dugout canoes for the Lake Bangweulu and

Zambesi river villages and trained half-caste or African operators, including one Cho—a splendid ex-Sergeant (I always recruited ex-soldiers if possible).

On the film side, the old original one-man chaos was reduced to something resembling order as more staff appeared. Some of them were even professionally qualified for the work.

However, broadcasting remained a terrible headache. We had now a real, though small, broadcasting station, with two large studios and offices and a transmitter house of optimistic proportions dwarfing two small transmitters with a combined output of two-and-a-half kilowatts, one of them from a second-hand transmitter bought for £150 from a ham in New York. (This one needed kicking as well.)

We opened the new studio with a flourish of invitations to tea on the lawn outside and a look round at the work going on inside—special programmes in both studios. A total breakdown was not inevitable, but I had prepared for the worst. I had told Louis to have everything set up for a sudden cinema show of travel films in the tea marquee if the worst happened. The length of the cable from his projector in the marquee was only just sufficient to get through a lavatory window on an outside wall of the studios and connect up with the light point therein.

Louis was to stay on watch at the marquee. In the event of real trouble I would tell the visitors, with a smile, that there was a film show going on in the marquee which they might like to see until we got back on the air again. When Louis saw our guests filing behind me towards the marquee he was to switch on the projector so that when we arrived, it would look as though the show was for anybody who got bored with the studios, not just an emergency precaution.

Everything was going splendidly in the studios, when the cautious Louis decided to switch on the projector in order to check the lavatory connection. It did not work. Nor did anything else. Everything in the broadcasting station went dead. The ex-railway telegraphist whom I had introduced to the company as my radio engineer, rushed hither and thither, testing things. I said there must be a break in the current somewhere. He said he knew that, and from the way he said it I thought I had better leave him alone for a time.

There were lots of cakes and sandwiches and tea left in the

marquee. I urged the guests to have another go at them. Time passed. I returned to the harassed engineer. He had found no fault in the studios or transmitter house.

'Then it must be outside' I said. 'The boiler in the town power station has bust again.'

'I've asked them' he said. 'Nothing's wrong there.'

'Then it must be in the outside cable. Where does it go from here?'

'Underground' he said.

'Where to?'

He shrugged despairingly.

A few visitors still lingered in the studios. One was a friend, a quantity surveyor in the PWD. I confided in him. He sympathized. Then a thought struck him.

'Bring me an axe' he said. 'I think I know where that cable goes.'

The other end of the cable was in a large metal sort of cupboard. The door was locked. It said, 'Keep Out. Danger. 3,000 Volts.' The quantity surveyor wielded the axe and opened the door. He pushed a trip-switch back into place and said, 'You overloaded the circuit. Switching on that projector was the last straw. That's what did it.' We went back to the studios: everything was working. Everybody had left.

'Lusaka Calling' continued its erratic call with staff that came and quickly went. There was a studio controller addicted to drink and another man who had had domestic trouble and decided to get away from it all. I met him on the plane and put him up for the night. At breakfast he said he had thought everything out and decided to return to his wife on the afternoon plane, which he did. I recruited a woman who had been an opera singer but had hysterics at the wrong times. Then came a cinema pianist and organist who had trekked in a lorry from London through Africa via the Sahara desert to Lusaka, where he got a job in the Public Works Department before coming to me.

I thought any man who had made that trek must be of sterling worth and I was right. He was a very good studio controller as well as an entertainer and put in a lot of overtime practising on our second-hand grand piano rehearsing his own programmes. He had the right attitude towards Africans, which was vital to the work. He was also a man of upright character. He went into the studio one night and found a couple locked in love on the studio carpet and reported this to me next morning.

'Something must be done about it' he said. 'What should we do?'

I thought it over and remembered the story of the Governor of another colony concerning a similar incident at a little country police station, where a young police officer had arranged to meet his girl when his office closed and to take her out for the evening. She arrived just as torrential tropical rain set in and was invited inside until it stopped. Love also set in; the office table was handy and the cessation of rain passed unnoticed. Unfortunately the Station Commander returned to the office at an awkward moment, for something he had forgotten, and reported the incident which went right up to the Chief Secretary. He decided that severe disciplinary measures must be taken. The Governor quashed the decision but directed that the officer be warned that Government furniture must not be used for such purposes in future . . . however inclement the weather.

I decided to do nothing about the affair on the studio carpet, having ascertained that the station had been off the air at the time so that no sounds of ecstasy could have reached the listening public.

The broadcasting service now began to improve rapidly. After a technical survey by a senior BBC engineer and the recruitment of an ex-BBC engineer, the station at last knew what it needed as far as transmitter coverage and studio equipment was concerned, though even our professional radio engineer was stumped when our enormous new transmitter arrived. It required enormous steel masts. There was still a world shortage of steel and no masts could be found.

I had seen wooden radio masts in South Africa; three or four trunks of tall eucalyptus trees bolted together and reaching quite a dizzy height. The South African Broadcasting Corporation railed the masts to us with the technical drawings showing how to erect them. The Director of Public Works had promised that his engineers would put up the masts. When they arrived his engineers studied them and the drawings and said it was an engineering impossibility. Any attempt would be most dangerous.

'Then we will put them up ourselves' I said defiantly.

'You will kill somebody if you try' they warned.

The broadcasting engineer said we would have to find an experienced rigger. There was no rigger.

With the aid of a Landrover and the entire broadcasting staff holding stays and ropes and the Landrover pulling the main rope the first mast started to rise until the driver was out of earshot of our screamed and conflicting instructions. Then there was a pause. Everything hovered and I clung to my stay and prayed. The driver decided to rely on his own initiative and went on—successfully. The masts went up and stayed up. It was dangerous and I should never have asked anybody to take the risk, but nobody minded. We were all enthusiastic amateurs—the Colonial Service was like that—and we all wanted to get those masts up.

We now had more or less adequate coverage, and before long we had adequate programmes. A new recruit from Johannesburg, who had spent some time with SABC and then recording African music for a company making gramophone records, proved to be so outstandingly good that I soon handed the station over to him. He ran it far better than I was able to. I only held the responsibility for it now.

Of course, there were still political troubles. Why was I turning the station into a broadcasting service for Africans? The Europeans wanted more of its time. What was to stop Africans listening to English broadcasts from Russia and other communist countries?

The answer to the second question might well have been that hardly any of them could listen to anything. They had no receivers and were much too poor to buy them. The cheapest receiver available locally was £45. Cost-cutting inventions such as the transistor were ten years off. I had tried England, America and even Australia, but nowhere could I find cheap receivers. We were now spending a lot of money on broadcasting to no, or very little, effect. Community receivers with loudspeakers blaring to the noisy crowd milling around the municipal beerhall were very little use even when they were working properly, which was not often. Nor were they much good at smaller rural centres. When their accumulators ran down they had to be taken to a town for recharging, and as they were nobody's responsibility except mine they stood and rotted unless one of my slender staff happened to be touring the area.

But the response from such small audiences that were able to listen to the receivers of benevolent Europeans was beyond even my expectations. They loved what they called the 'wayaleshi' (wireless). It was wonderful white man's magic, and for once it was for them.

It was incredible magic to a crowd of Barotse tribesmen listening to a District Commissioner's set one evening. There had been a by-election to fill a seat on the Paramount Chief's lower council. The votes had been sent to Provincial Headquarters for counting and they had telegraphed the results to me just before the Barotse News came on. I passed the telegram over to the studio.

I had earlier given the Barotse News reader a letter from one of his compatriots giving us some information on the candidates and his comments and predictions on the election. I had told the news reader to extract only the candidates' names from the letter and to add a few lines about when the result was expected and so on. The announcer thought it would be easier to read out the letter, including a passage which referred to one candidate as a drunken old man with a beard like a goat and a stink like a goat, always interfering with women. There was a little more in this vein and the writer concluded: 'The people will not vote for a goat.'

In the event they did not. The District Commissioner wrote, 'Laughter changed to a stunned silence when the name of the successful candidate was read out. I don't know how you did it myself, but as far as the people are concerned, it was more astounding than anything a witchdoctor could do.'

Letters that we received from a few literate listeners were almost pathetically grateful and from them it seemed that we had got the proportions of news and instructive talks to entertainment about right but some alterations in the kinds of entertainment were needed. I found the letters more depressing than cheering. The fact that radio was doing for a few hundred people what I had always believed it would only made my failure to find any source of cheap receivers more frustrating. Fortunately neither the officials nor the unofficials in the Government realized how few listeners we had, and I did not propose to tell them yet. But were I ever to be challenged in the Budget Committee on this aspect, Lusaka Radio might have been cut out of the Estimates. There were plenty of other services, particularly the medical service, which could have done with the extra money and made better use of it than we were doing.

The Saucepan

Early in 1948 I went on leave. Before I left I told the senior broadcasting staff that if I could find no answer to this problem in England I would not be justified in keeping the service going. I asked the radio engineer to prepare drawings and specifications of a suitable receiver, cutting out all frills, such as a tone control. The set would have to be strong enough to survive two or three weeks at sea, four days on a goods train, hundreds of miles of potholed earth road and probably rough treatment by its owner. The cabinet was to be of metal; plastic was not yet in use and a wooden cabinet in a village hut could be destroyed by white ants in a night while its owner slept. Any necessary openings in the receiver were to be covered with fine wire gauze to keep out the insects, large and small, with which Africa is plagued. Simplicity of operation and easy access for repair work and tropicalization of components were essential. It had, of course, to be dry-battery operated as there was no electricity supply to any African huts either in towns or villages.

In London I talked to representatives of all the major manufacturers of receivers. I told them that there was an enormous market waiting for cheap receivers, not only in the non-white countries of the Empire but in all the impoverished undeveloped countries of the world. They would not believe it and produced all the arguments against it that I had been given in my search by correspondence from Lusaka.

I gave up, but kept thinking and remembered an attractive redhead, former wife of a doctor friend in Broken Hill, who was said to have married the chairman of the Ever Ready Company in London. I looked up his name, Magnus Goodfellow, and rang his house. He was out, but his wife listened sympathetically to my story and said 'Come round tomorrow and meet him over a drink.'

'I don't think there's really any chance of him doing what I want' I said. 'Nobody else will.'

'I'll talk him into it' she answered.

Ever Ready were not primarily a radio manufacturing company but they made some receivers as an extra outlet for their major product, dry batteries, and I should have thought of them before. The way to tackle the chairman was on the Gillette razor and the blade principle: sell the receivers at cost and leave the profit to the resulting expansion of the battery trade.

Magnus Goodfellow was one of the last of the old-type captains of industry. He was more than chairman, he virtually ran the company. He was a hard tycoon of business, but the type of man that would do anything he wanted and be damned, and twice damned if everybody else said it could not be done.

I went to a nice little champagne party at his house. His wife sang and he played the piano. Goodfellow appeared to like the idea of bringing some light to darkest Africa through dry battery receivers. When I envied his Rolls Royce and told him I had never been in one, he offered to drive me home to Kent in it.

'We'll all go' he said '. . . see the dawn.'

The next day he still liked my idea, as an idea, but there was no champagne to overcome the doubts that had crept into his mind about the potential market.

'You said the average income of these poor devils was less than five pounds a year. No wonder you limit the retail price of the receiver to a fiver: they come to over six pounds with the battery. How many can afford that?'

I explained that this was the average *cash* income, that food and housing cost them nothing and that although the village subsistence peasants earned practically nothing, employed men earned about £25 p.a. on average and brought some money back to villages after two or three years working in the towns. Several thousand of them had bought bicycles, several thousand could buy a cheap receiver. If we sold only a thousand that would give us at least ten thousand listeners.

'They are a gregarious people' I said, 'and they share what they have. Every village or compound hut with a radio will invite the neighbours in until the walls bend. And what they hear will get around the villages without a radio. African life is like that.'

'Tell us exactly what you want and we'll see,' said Magnus Goodfellow. (He was well named.)

Once one person decides to help, others follow. It seems to be a law of life. A top BBC engineer, Bill Varley, vetted my engineer's drawings and specifications for the set, made a few minor improvements and agreed to come with me to an Ever Ready directors' lunch and talk to the company's radio expert.

I was almost shaking with suspense. I knew I had put much too good a story of the business prospects of the scheme and facing the board of directors of a big company with a Rolls Royced chairman who, his secretary told me, did not suffer fools gladly and had a terrible temper, was beyond my experience.

Bill Varley, who was to rise right to the top of his profession, talked radio technology to his Ever Ready counterpart after lunch, while I tried to impress the other directors. I had not yet realized that it mattered little whether or not they were impressed, so long as Magnus was.

Magnus saw me off the premises with a few encouraging words. 'We'll make a few prototypes' he said. 'It won't take long. I'll send a man out with them to investigate the market.'

Some weeks later I went back to the boardroom with Bill to see two prototypes. One was round, the other square. I chose the round one: if it was accidentally dropped it would roll instead of smashing a corner.

The cabinet was made of aluminium alloy. Bill said it looked like a saucepan without a handle.

'That's what it is,' said Magnus. 'There's a saucepan factory up the road. The square one's a biscuit tin. We'll make a dozen samples of the round one. What shall we call it?'

'The Saucepan Radio' suggested Bill, grinning. To his surprise Magnus and I agreed. It was a good joke that turned out to be a brilliant idea.

The Ever Ready market investigator brought the samples to Lusaka and spent some time collecting statistics. He was enthusiastic about the project but not about the statistics, which indicated that there was no market at all for the Saucepan Radio. He said he was sad about it, but that he would have to report to Magnus accordingly. I had never cared much about statistics and said so.

'You haven't seen anything of the country or the people yet.' I said. 'Come with me about three hundred miles up the Great North Road, to the Copperbelt. We'll stop at random and distribute the samples on the way. You can have a look round the copper mines and then on the way back you can hear what people think of the radios.'

I had travelled over the Great North Road hundreds of times. Our stops were not quite at random. There was a man with a little store outside Broken Hill and further on an enterprising villager who had extended his peasant holding into a small farm, and others that I knew could afford to buy the Saucepan.

We set the receivers up for them, with earth and aerial wires and showed them how to operate the sets. 'Five pounds for the set and twenty-five shillings for the battery,' we said, 'if you decide to buy.'

On the way back our welcome was a door-to-door salesman's dream. Most of the sets were paid for on the spot, the others would pay when they could raise the cash. But the market investigator was still not satisfied.

'One swallow doesn't make a summer' he reflected, 'and you seemed to know those chaps pretty well.'

'The Government will buy fifteen hundred sets. I can get an imprest and pay it back when the sets are sold' I said hopefully, wondering how the Treasury would react to the idea of the Government going into the retail trade.

That tipped the scales. Ever Ready got busy. The Treasury was more amused than shocked. The railway telegraphist came into his own since he knew how to check and trim receivers. His office was so crammed with them that he only just had enough space to wield a screwdriver. The sets were sold as fast as he could trim them.

I had thought that they might be met with some suspicion at first, but there was none, although one owner wrote as follows: '*When taking the radio from the store with its ordinary saucepan's colour, I had not any hope of it being a useful and interesting thing. Before 5 p.m. of that day we were discussing with my wife and family that we have just lost our money for nothing. The hour came, it was 5pm. I started operating. It came like thunder in our ears. At the same time we all laughed. It made us to forget our £6-5-0 of which we thought was lost in the water.*'

This was a start, but obviously a commercial distributor would have to take over future supplies, and it would not be easy to find one interested in selling things at a negligible profit. Fortunately the local director of the London-based company that controlled a large slice of the retail trade of the Protectorate was another Magnus, and he solved our problem.

Thus we pioneered African broadcasting, in the same way, though with a different objective, that others before us had pioneered the continent itself; by taking one step forward to get a better look at the next step without worrying about what it might look like when we reached it.

We had had the backing of the Colonial Office from the start and after the first few years of our broadcasting efforts, Whitehall, never having seen how chaotic they were, had begun to urge other colonies to follow our example. Those that could afford the expense, did; many could not.

Some were now at the 'station cat' stage, others had moved further. All were faced with the same problem—no listeners. The Saucepan Radio was the answer, and it began to sell in other parts of the Empire. They found a market as far off as the Tonga Islands, where the Queen of Tonga bought a hundred to distribute among her 45,000 subjects, presumably to enable them to listen to New Zealand which was their nearest broadcasting station, some two thousand miles away.

Our Lusaka station and the Saucepan Radio now came in for much publicity in Britain and even in Europe and America. A radio built inside a saucepan seemed to stimulate the imagination of every visiting writer and foreign correspondent.

The impact of the Saucepan Radio on African life was even greater than I had anticipated. Letters from listeners changed from a trickle to a flow. They thanked us; they thanked the Northern Rhodesia Government, the British Government, the Governor and the King. They thanked '*those kind people in England who took pains in considering the production of these cheap wireless sets.*'

They also thanked God: '*My fellow Africans, let us praise God for His kindness He has done to us. Long ago we Africans were not suspected to buy such a big thing, but by now we are lucky in possessing these "sets" and talk* (he meant listen) *to each other as of same village.*'

The letters came in from both English and vernacular literates and from illiterates who got someone to write for them. Happiness was a major theme.

'*To me every evening is a jolly evening and makes home a happy home*' wrote one; and another, more emotionally, '*Oh! How very happy we are, I and my wife Lucy. How very pleased we are when our wireless starts to speak at five o'clock.*' One correspondent burst into capitals, '*For ages I have been feeling lonely. Now I have the WHOLE WORLD in my house.*'

To some this happiness was a counter to less worthy leisure pursuits. One proud owner wrote, with reforming zeal, '*To the Beer Drinkers I am to say that if they are to buy this machine instead of spending 1/6d or more daily on beer, they will find no time for that.*' Another advised '*If you have bad thoughts in you or are fond of fighting others, when you get your own set and listen in you can forget and stop all your bad ways.*

Nowadays I will be enjoying a lot if I don't die quickly.' That ending was probably neither a joke nor a foreboding; Africans, like Arabs, never tempt the gods to destroy.

Our educational programmes were highly valued. Village schoolteachers were using their sets in school and reported on their usefulness. Letters like '*These sets are real teachers,*' or '*Now I have a teacher in my home,*' were typical. Others discussed the contents of the programmes or made suggestions concerning them. '*The people*' wrote Chief Shinde, '*desire to hear more about care of dams and how water can be usefully reserved during the whole year.*'

There must have been many to whom these programmes meant very little, but they could at least follow our impromptu and unrehearsed plays. A travelling Orderly of the Water Department who, like many others, took his Saucepan with him wherever he went, wrote '*I met six men with their wives. They asked me to open my wireless, if they could hear what was going on here. The first play was about Malikopo, when he burnt the grain bin because they thought this man Malikopo had a lot of food when they were suffering from lack of it. The second part was about Malikopo killing a child. Here too, women were very sorry and one even cried and ran away and promised not to return any more. This made us laugh very much.*'

My guess that we could count on ten listeners per receiver seemed an under-estimate. Disregarding enthusiasts who claimed to have hundreds of listeners every night, it was plain that whenever a Saucepan was switched on people listened outside the hut as well as inside and that their owners gained many new friends—'who even come when it is not the right time to listen,' one correspondent recorded. Wherever a Saucepan travelled, and with lorry drivers they travelled far, people gathered round. Wayside storekeepers kept their sets on all day, to attract customers, transmitting music from Lourenço Marques until we came on the air.

A Provincial Education Officer, camped in the Barotse plains, in a letter painting a picture that I could so easily see, wrote '*By about 8 p.m. over a hundred people were present, with many children, who should have been in bed, in the foreground: the Silalo Induna* (sub-chief) *sitting on a chair amongst them, the women and men behind, in a semicircle. I shall never forget the look of rapture on a blind man's face as he listened to the programmes. He came every time I had it on.*

'*One child of about four sat smiling for about two hours, its face literally smothered in flies. The women joined in the songs and thoroughly enjoyed themselves.'*

As usual, I learnt by experience. I suggested to radio owners that as batteries would have to be renewed sometime, they might keep a battery fund, a little tin into which their listener friends might sometimes drop a penny or two. 'That is not according to our custom,' I was rebuked. 'It would shame us.'

I learnt that Africans were no longer almost exclusively interested in local and tribal affairs. They wanted to read and hear more about other parts of the territory, other countries in Africa and in Europe. Something new was stirring in their minds and hearts. Their letters sometimes referred to 'living in a new environment', to 'waking up', to 'the modern world', to 'the new world'. *'Though some of us are very poor and worthless,* (the writer meant without possessions) *but yet we bought our dignity through the wireless sets which the European brought to all Africans.'* In one respect at least that correspondent was equal to the white man (and that was what he wanted); he owned a radio.

CHAPTER FIFTEEN

Swan Song for A Phoenix

WE TRIED to keep politics (and until now that had simply meant white politics) out of broadcasting as much as possible, and out of all other aspects of our work. The time came when we had to try to keep out African politics too. The Africans knew what was going on. Those who were literate in English read the newspapers that came up from Southern Rhodesia and also the paper that Roy Welensky had started on the Copperbelt, the *Northern News*. The bush telegraph spread the words to the villages and the further they spread the more sensational they became, as far as white politics were concerned.

On the surface, there was little for the newspapers to report about African politics. There were two Africans in the Legislative Council but they said very little; there was the African Representative Council, set up in 1946 to advise the Governor on any matters affecting Africans (a meaningless phrase, since anything of any importance that went on in the territory affected them); and there was the modest and polite nucleus of the African National Congress Party taking shape on the Copperbelt.

The African Representative Council, which nominated the two Africans in Legislative Council for the Governor's approval, consisted of thirty representatives, chiefs and local worthies. The Secretary for Native Affairs was chairman of the Council. The representatives were chosen by African Provincial Councils whose chairmen, the Provincial Commissioners, had to approve their appointment. The African Representative Council did not therefore greatly resemble a ball of fire, nor could its members be considered 'agitators'. It nevertheless made its feelings known on the subject of the white settlers' ambition to rule. It made these feelings known with pleading, not with aggression, and they were feelings with which the Secretary for Native Affairs and the Provincial Commissioners were entirely sympathetic.

But politics were not regarded as 'matters affecting Africans'. The Representative Council could pass a resolution recommending to the Governor the abolition of bicycle licences, but it could hardly be allowed to cause a major row in the Legislative and Executive Councils between the official and unofficial members, with repercussions in Westminster and Whitehall, by a resolution recommending the removal of the white settler politicians to a far place.

Roy Welensky replaced Sir Stewart Gore-Browne, after the war, as Leader of the 'white settler' members of the Legislative Council. Sir Stewart had never been acceptable to them because he was the nominated member appointed to represent African interests. His political experience and his well-trained mind had been of great value to Welensky, but the latter's powerful personality, drive and white rule objective made him the natural leader. He never formed a political party: there was no need for one. His colleagues in the Legislature were men of little calibre and they were all Welensky's men, overshadowed by him and commanded by him.

Roy Welensky was in a hurry to get away from Colonial Office rule, as he frequently proclaimed. In a debate in 1946 he warned the House 'that by 1968, if the present policy continues, there will be an elected African majority here'. He went on to express his belief that the black man would not be ready for 'our form of government' within the next twenty years. He was right, but neither he nor the Colonial Office nor the Colonial Service ever did much to prepare the Africans for self-government, and the more Welensky proclaimed his objective the more frightened did the Africans become and the more receptive to the growing African Nationalist movement.

In 1947 and 1948, Welensky's speeches became stronger. 'The time has come for the European population to oppose the Colonial Office policy with everything in their power,' he proclaimed. He now wanted the amalgamation of Northern Rhodesia with the white settler governed Southern Rhodesia (he was a Southern Rhodesian himself) which, he thought, would be a quicker way to reach his end.

I was too engrossed in developing mass education to worry about these speeches, and thought the white politicians were just letting off steam. But I was wrong. I soon realized that Roy Welensky was a much more formidable figure than I had thought.

His power continued to increase. The white politicians, in 1948, demanded 'responsible government' without delay and threatened to 'paralyse or partially paralyse' the Government by using such powers as they already possessed. It was not an entirely empty threat. Had they attempted to carry it out Northern Rhodesia would have had to revert to the Governor's rule of nearly a generation back, and that would have horrified the British Government since it would have resulted in the need to abandon the pretence of democratic rule in the colonies; and that was something which it wished earnestly to preserve.

It was for that reason that the attitude of the Colonial Office to Roy Welensky and his followers had gradually changed during the mid-forties. The change was naturally reflected in the attitude of at least some of the senior official members of the Northern Rhodesia Government. Keep the peace with the elected members; it saves a lot of trouble.

Welensky, ever more vigorous, was faithfully performing the task for which he had been elected—the move towards eventual white settler rule. At the same time, I was performing mine—to help to bring the Africans up to the stage when they could stand on their own feet and the protecting power could hand over the reins to them. That aim was implicit in the treaties by which the Protectorate had been established. Neither I nor any of my colleagues thought the handover would be in our time, but that in no way modified the fact that it was the objective to which we were working.

By the very nature of its work, the Information Department was always in the public eye and by the same nature it was a department which could, were it under his control or influence, considerably help Roy Welensky towards *his* objectives. Frequent clashes with him were almost inevitable. Both he and Sir Stewart Gore-Browne were now members of Executive Council (the Cabinet). Both had declined portfolios and thus could concentrate on their politics. I was sometimes called to Executive Council to answer their questions, particularly concerning broadcasting. I was used to appearing in Executive Council when it consisted of the Governor representing the Crown and his top Colonial Service official advisers to discuss my Department and its needs (particularly financial) or to advise on publicity arrangements for major events, such as the visit of the Royal Family to Livingstone, but I felt that I had come to

Northern Rhodesia to serve the Crown and the Africans and not local white politicians. Roy Welensky knew that and could hardly be expected to like it any more than I would have liked it, had our positions been reversed. Our hostility was natural and mutual.

I was given a tip-off that he was going to break the Information Department at the Budget meeting of Legislative Council. I was called into the Budget Committee, a committee of the whole House, taking with me the files on the subjects on which I thought he would attack. I also put a sheet of foolscap paper in my inside pocket. It was the draft of a leader I had written for *Mutende* some months back, and on it were some valuable comments by another hand. It had been a difficult leader to write and not wanting yet another political row—I was getting fed up with rows—I had sent the draft to Sir Stewart Gore-Browne, the unofficial member representing African interests. I had asked him for his, and Welensky's comments and suggestions. The two were close friends and were known to us as the 'Terrible Twins'. Sir Stewart had returned the draft noting that Welensky had refused to comment on it, saying instead that the leader would give him more ammunition with which to attack me in the House. Welensky had not expected Sir Stewart to pass that information on to me.

Early in the proceedings Welensky launched a vigorous attack on the leader. I protested. He had had the opportunity to amend the draft.

Sir Stewart, who had kept silent until then, said cunningly, 'I don't suppose you have kept that draft, have you?'

I produced it from my pocket, but nobody wanted to see it. It had already had its effect. I left the Budget Committee with my estimates slightly increased after one unofficial member, a missionary, asked, without opposition, if I was sure there was nothing more I needed.

However, the frequent clashes with one or other of the white politicians were beginning to wear me down. I had always been backed up by the head of the Civil Service, the Chief Secretary, who was also Leader of the House and as a rule I usually still was. But I could no longer rely on that: on several occasions I had not received that support.

The old policy, of 'Don't worry about the politicians', was now replaced by 'We must all get on better with the politicians, work together with them.' But this could not alter the fact that we remained the trustees of our 'protected' people. How could we work with the protagonists of white settler rule? Soon perhaps we should be expected to work for, not with, the white politicians. It looked as though they might be going to take over after all.

The prospect depressed me as it depressed most of my colleagues in the Colonial Service of the Protectorate. Most of all it depressed the Africans.

The beginnings of African Nationalist politics were basically defensive, springing from the fear of the increasing power of the white politicians. They were not yet against Colonial Office rule and were of little account while the people felt that the Colonial Office, the British Government, would never let them down by handing over their country to the white settlers.

The African National Congress lacked leadership and was so ill-organized that it could scarcely be called a political party. A few individuals from the educated class had formed branches here and there but these followed no uniform policy. Each had gathered a small following, and the more Welensky's power grew the more friends they found. The white politicians' threat to paralyse the Government had played straight into their hands. Why had the Government not thrown these people out of the Legislative Council? And what did this new threat about amalgamating Northern Rhodesia with the white settler-governed Southern Rhodesia mean?

In reply to the demand for responsible government by the white politicians in Legislative Council, the Chief Secretary of the day had declined to comment on the proposal, saying that it was merely a prelude to Amalgamation (as indeed it was).

Amalgamation of the two Rhodesias was not on. It had been proposed occasionally over the years by the Southern Rhodesia Government and the white settler representatives in Northern Rhodesia. On each occasion the chiefs, African welfare societies and similar organizations had emphatically opposed it, realizing that it would mean white settler domination of the North just like that already existing in the South. They wanted to be ruled by the 'King in England', as they expressed it.

Since the war both Sir Godfrey Huggins (later Lord Malvern), as Prime Minister of Southern Rhodesia, and Roy Welensky—soon to be Sir Roy—had continually pressed for Amalgamation.

After the attempted demarche early in 1948 events had moved rapidly and the Africans, no longer feeling that they could rely on the Colonial Service and the British Government to save them from white domination, turned more to the African National Congress. It found a leader and became more cohesive.

Later in 1948, following a Conference at the Victoria Falls of the politicians from the North and the South on the Amalgamation issue, Roy Welensky and Sir Godfrey went to London. The Colonial Secretary, the late Arthur Creech Jones (Lab.), made it quite plain that Amalgamation could never be considered, but later dropped a hint that proposals for a Federation, which would include Nyasaland, would at least be looked at. So Federation became the demand of the whites. The Africans thought it was the same thing as Amalgamation, and in this they were not far wrong.

From now on, every political action by the British and the Northern Rhodesia Governments played into the hands of the African Nationalist Party. It soon became the rallying ground for many Africans in rural areas as well as those in the towns. Many others disliked the Party and the way it behaved but none were against its objectives; no white settler rule, and no Federation. All its members were confused about what the British Government's intentions really were. I was too. Although I was convinced that Federation would never come about, I thought that the white politicians *would* soon control the Government of Northern Rhodesia, with Roy Welensky as Prime Minister. In the event, it was the other way round.

Changes of command at the top did not help to clear the confusion. Sir John Waddington retired in 1948 and a new Chief Secretary was appointed as Acting Governor until the arrival of Sir Gilbert Rennie. Sir Gilbert was a very able man, but even the ablest of men take a little time to settle down in a strange territory.

Early in 1949 the British Government said it would not close its mind to the idea of Federation. In November, Roy Welensky proposed a motion in the House, 'That the time is opportune for His Majesty's Government to take the lead in creating a Federal African State.' The Colonial Service officials of the Legislative Council, on instructions from London, did not oppose the motion. They walked out after the Chief Secretary had said 'We cannot vote for the motion. We are not satisfied that the time is opportune. But a vote against the motion would be regarded by many as a vote against Federation and the Government has an open mind on the question of Federation.' The field was left to Welensky.

The officials who walked out, together with the four African representatives who stayed to vote against, could have killed the motion. The African intelligentsia knew that, and what they knew the bush telegraph spread through the towns and villages of the territory: the ranks of the African National Congress multiplied accordingly and some underground political agitation began.

The Labour Party quite liked the idea of the Federation (the Conservatives liked it even more) provided that it included Nyasaland and that the Africans consented to it. It was thought that the two black protectorates together would be able to hold their own against the white-dominated Southern Rhodesia. Neither party seemed to realize that the Africans would be quite unable to hold their own against Southern Rhodesia and that nothing on earth would ever persuade them to consent to the Federation. They knew that the white politicians of the two Protectorates were already too powerful and could foresee white domination spreading up from the south very fast once a Federation was created. The British Government's failure to realize this was why it had proclaimed that its mind was not closed to the idea of Federation.

Now the Secretary of State for the Colonies, the Right Hon. Arthur Creech Jones came out to tour Northern Rhodesia and learn more about it. He was an honest man, with his heart in the right place. I went round the country with him, and dutifully avoided talking politics, home or colonial, with him. My job was to brief him on any facts he might need to know. The Colonial Office had already briefed him, but their facts were not always the same as ours.

There was a rowdy meeting of white miners on the Copperbelt shouting about Colonial Office coddling of the Africans, which Mr Creech Jones handled very well. He told them that they were about the best-paid miners in the world and the Africans were the worst-paid. However, his reply to criticisms that Britain was taking money out of Northern Rhodesia was not correct, even though he thought it was. He was thinking of local taxation when he indignantly denied the charges. In fact Britain was getting at least several million pounds from taxing London-based companies like the

British South Africa Company, which levied royalties on all the mines and had large investments in some of them, and from British shareholders of the mining companies. In addition Britain enjoyed considerable indirect trading benefits.

Like all politicians, Mr Creech Jones shook hands with everybody within reach, wherever he went, which rather startled but pleased itinerant Africans. They had no idea who he was but welcomed him as a white man with no colour bar. During his tour we visited an African School for the Blind near Fort Jameson where a mad ex-askari was employed as a sweeper. Mr Creech Jones got out of the wrong side of the car. The reception committee was lined up on the other side. Only the sweeper was visible so the Secretary of State shook his hand and asked who he was. The sweeper saluted smartly and said, 'Me, Kingy George'.

Unfortunately an election was imminent in Britain and Mr Creech Jones lost his seat. There was no doubt whose side he was on and he would never have agreed to the Federation without the consent of the Africans. Nor, in the event, did the Labour Party. But the new Labour Government did not last long and during its short time in office it made a valuable concession to Roy Welensky and to the Prime Minister of Southern Rhodesia by agreeing in 1950 to set up a Commission of expert senior officials to study, in London, the practical possibilities of Federation. It was from the report of that Commission that the Federation ultimately stemmed. There had never been any doubt that the practicalities of Federation could be worked out on paper. The doubt was (and to me it had always been more than a doubt) whether it could work in the teeth of total African opposition, and overcome that opposition by the benefits which a white settler government would bring to the African people. It did not so work. It was a disaster and was broken up within ten years. The after-effects of its creation are still evident in the Rhodesian rebellion.

But then, in 1950, what would happen was still uncertain. What was certain (or so it seemed to me) was that either increasing white political power in Northern Rhodesia or total white political power in a Federation spelled the end of the policy of the paramountcy of African interests. That was a policy which was already crumbling and it was the only policy under which I felt I could work.

More important perhaps, it had been the stated policy of the

British Government ever since 1930, and when Africans in the 1940s had expressed their fears that the white settlers looked like succeeding in gaining control of the Protectorate, the Colonial Service administrators in the central government and in the field had always reassured them—or tried to reassure them—that this would never happen. By the end of the 1940s our instructions were to assure them that Federation would never happen without their consent. But it began to look as though it would. If it did we would presumably have to tell them what a splendid thing it was. I knew that the main agency used to spread the good news would be the Information Department, and Lusaka Radio in particular. (That is exactly what eventually happened.) What would they think of us?

What were they already thinking of us? A great deal had been happening in the last year or two that we had not reported either from the broadcasting station or in *Mutende*. There had been a conference of the politicians of Northern and Southern Rhodesia at the Victoria Falls in which the Prime Minister of Southern Rhodesia had made it clear that his idea of Federation was virtually the absorption of the North by the South. There had been continual attacks by the politicians in the Northern Rhodesian Legislative Council upon the Colonial Office and the Colonial Service Government, whose control was already weakened. There had been speeches about the Africans' role in the future, one of which (not made by Roy Welensky, who I believe strongly disapproved of it) in effect threatened that much of their land would be taken away from them as they could not work it. Land, to any peasant, is life, regardless of whether or not he has more of it than he can work, and nothing can be more calculated to stir up trouble than a threat to take some of it away from him.

Our Department of Information and Broadcasting was a Civil Service department. We could not report these things. There was no such restriction upon the European press and so they became known, and we began receiving from listeners letters that we could not answer.

I thought the situation over and decided that I could not, would not, stay in the Service. But how could I afford to leave it after twenty-one years, without a pension, and what sort of job could an ex-administrator Jack-of-all-trades-and-master-of-none get? Under the existing conditions of service I could retire on pension at forty-five but I was only forty-four. In a few months' time those conditions were to be replaced and the retiring age would be fifty-five. Too bad. Then I discovered that, in some mysterious way that I never quite understood, I could add to my age the fourteen months accumulated leave that I had never had time to take, put in my resignation, go on leave and then on pension at the end of it.

What would I do then? What did I want to do? I wanted to do what I had been doing—to bring broadcasting to poor and under-developed peoples who had never heard it. I was on UNESCO's panel of alleged experts in various fields whom they could call on for advice. I had given them some, free, on what they called 'Poor Man's Radio'. Perhaps they would like some more—and be prepared to pay for it. Or Ever Ready, co-pioneers of Poor Man's Radio, might give me a job to extend the pioneering?

Civil servants are cautious types. I took a four days' leave and flew to Paris and London. In Paris, UNESCO said, 'Later, perhaps' while in London, Ever Ready gave the answer 'Now'. I bought thirty-five acres of Crown land in the hills outside Lusaka for £25 down and about £5 a year for 999 years—just in case. A man can always live off the land. Farming would probably be easy enough, and if it proved not to be I could always make bricks or build wooden bridges for somebody.

So I put in my resignation and left a few weeks later, at the end of November 1951. The farewell staff party was held in one of the broadcasting studios in an atmosphere that did not exist outside it. Broadcasting really had broken down barriers, at least among the European and African staff engaged in it. The old autocracy, the old paternalism, had changed. We were friends at a mixed party of black and white.

On the miserable train journey down to Cape Town, I tried to console myself with the thought that the Information Department was now solidly established and its broadcasting was in more capable hands than mine: that was true enough but no consolation, especially if it was going to be misused.

I took the slowest possible boat home from Cape Town, for a last lingering look at Africa. It took seven weeks by the long East coast route, which I had never travelled on before, and stopped at every little port.

Everywhere the picture was the same: a minority holding all the wealth, privilege and power, and a massive majority with not much more materially than the means to exist, but at least to exist in peace. There was a certain inevitability about the situation. It would take, I thought, half a century or more before these peoples could achieve western standards of living, of education, of civilization. But they would, I reflected rather bitterly as we slowly chugged back to England, be further along the road—might by now even have reached its end—if the people of Britain had been sufficiently interested to see to it that more money had been provided by their governments to take them along that road.

And what had I done? Well, something helpful, I supposed, as we all had in the Colonial Service, the Indian Civil Service, the Sudan Service. We were, after all, paid to do something helpful.

The past was already beginning to seem like a dream. What was there left to show that it was real? An inscribed copper replica of the Saucepan Radio, made on the mines, one of the presents from the staff. An OBE (we called it Other Buggers' Efforts in the Service and had equally disrespectful names for the other degrees of the order) which, as a flag-wagger, I was pleased about. My mother would like it too: she could come to Buckingham Palace to see the King give it to me. Some farewell letters from Africans. They were the reality, they were the reassurance and what they wrote they meant. They used no long, smooth words.

The ship rolled and pitched through the Indian Ocean, much as the *Glengorm Castle* had rolled and pitched through the Atlantic, until I woke one night and she seemed to have stopped. I looked out of the porthole. She was moving, quietly, slowly, across a moonlit desert. There was no sea, only an occasional light that looked as though it was within reach of my arm. It was the Suez canal, and my last look at Africa.

I should never have left Northern Rhodesia, I thought. I had loved the country, the great space and quiet of it, its colours, the smell of the first rains on its parched baked earth, the tinkle of a kalimba as the man who had fashioned it picked at the little metal strips as he walked along, making up his own private tune. If I had not loved its people—what does it mean, to love a whole people, you can't, nobody can—at least I had liked them as a teacher likes his pupils.

In London I should join the ants, hurrying from their crowded nests of bricks and mortar, joining in orderly columns as they approached the tunnel that would take them underground to their work, streaming out of it at the other end and jostling, bumping into each other as they dispersed to forage, to work for their food. I should never see Northern Rhodesia again.

It did not happen that way. I came back.

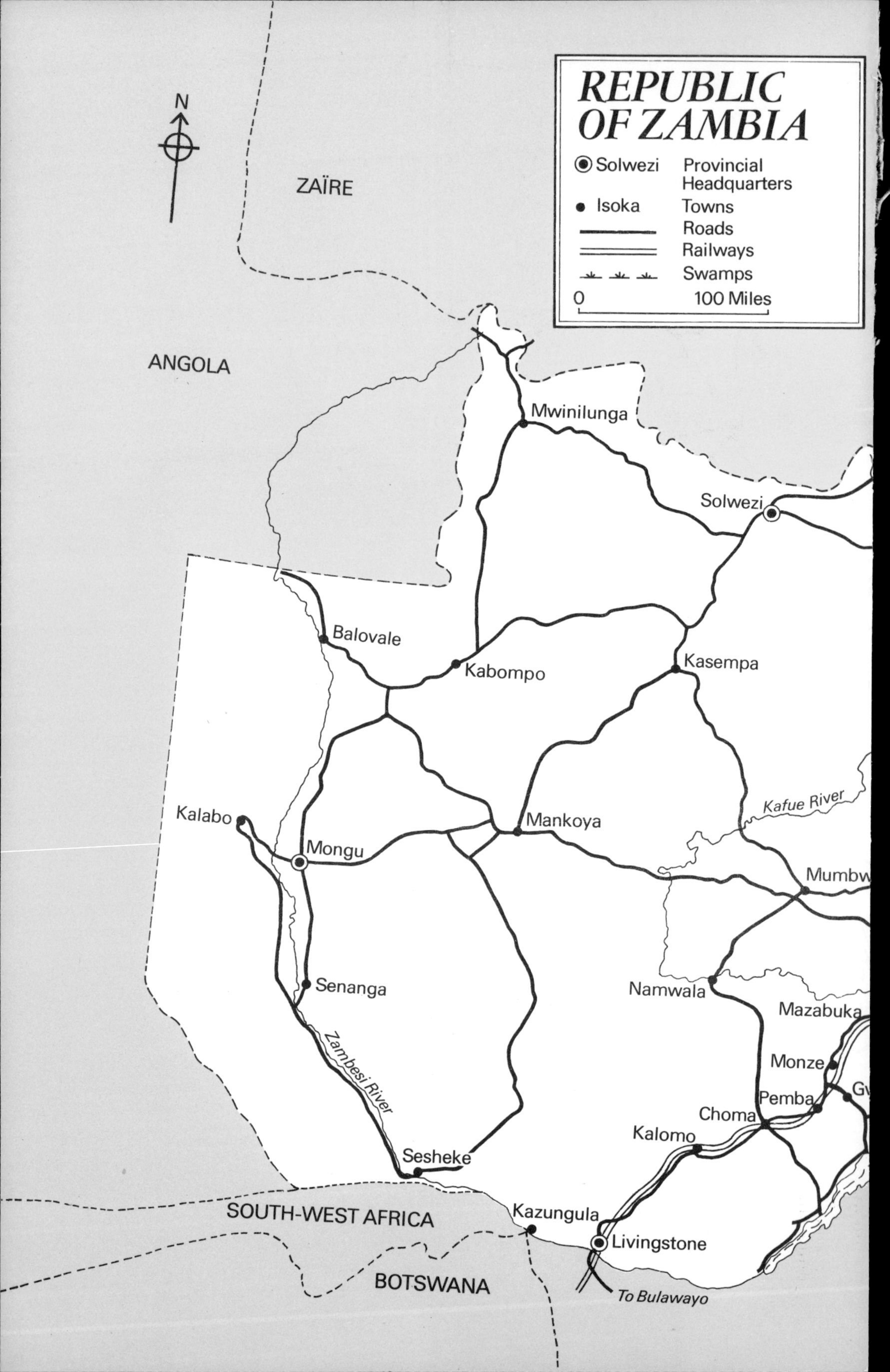

REPUBLIC OF ZAMBIA
Solwezi Provincial Headquarters
Isoka Towns
Roads
Railways
Swamps
0 100 Miles
N
ZAÏRE
ANGOLA
Mwinilunga
Solwezi
Balovale
Kabompo
Kasempa
Kafue River
Kalabo
Mankoya
Mongu
Mumbw
Namwala
Senanga
Mazabuka
Zambesi River
Monze
Pemba
Choma
Kalomo
Sesheke
SOUTH-WEST AFRICA
Kazungula
Livingstone
BOTSWANA
To Bulawayo